SPITTING
IN THE WIND

SPITTING IN THE WIND

The True Story Behind The Violent Legacy of The Black Panther Party

By Earl Anthony

ROUNDTABLE
Publishing, Inc.

HV 7911 .A64 A3 1989
Anthony, Earl.
Spitting in the wind

SPITTING IN THE WIND. Copyright© 1990 by Earl Anthony. All rights reserved. Printed in the United States of America. No part of this book may be used or reproduced in any manner whatsoever without written permission except in the cases of brief quotations embodied in critical articles or reviews. For information, address Rountable Publishing Company, 29169 Heathercliff Road Malibu, CA 90265.

Cover design by Mitch Burkhardt

Library of Congress Cataloging-in-Publication Data

Anthony, Earl, 1940-

   Spitting in the wind/by Earl Anthony.

  1. Anthony, Earl, 1940 Biography. 2. Informers—United States—Biography. 3. Black Panther Party. 4. Black Muslims—United States. 5. United States. Federal Bureau of Investigation. 6. United States. Central Intelligence Agency. 7. Title.

HV7911.A64A3	1989	89-24310cip
ISBN 0-915677-45-8		363.2'52'092—dc20

To my daughter,
Maat Kamilah Anthony
And in memory of my father,
James Willard Anthony
1920-1988

Author's Preface

It was with total sincerity that I joined the Black Panther Party in April of 1967. I had been moving (in one way or another) toward coming to grips with the way things were for blacks in American society for some time and was looking for a solution to the problems as I saw them. The way I saw American society and the place I saw it from probably will not fit your idea of of a "black militant."

As I stated in my earlier book about the Panthers, *Picking Up The Gun*, published in 1970: "I had become totally disenchanted with the course of American politics."

I'm not sure when this disenchantment was "totally" realized in my own mind; certainly while a student at the University of Southern California, I came to realize that in the United States there was, and is, too often a direct relationship between the color of your face and the amount of money in your bank account. Still, I did graduate from that institution as a member of the Young Republicans, who had supported Barry Goldwater's presidential campaign in 1964.

Sometimes afterwards, not long after I moved to San Francisco to attend law school, it dawned on me that something was wrong with this society, and it wasn't anything the Republicans or the Democrats were going to willingly change. Something was basically wrong in a society where there was so much poverty that was not being seriously addressed by anyone.

It was for that reason that I became involved in the San Francisco rent strikes as a law student; became the leader of the rent strike movement and that led to me being introduced to the Black Panther Party. At that time, the BBP was only a few months old and consisted of founders Bobby Seale and Huey Newton, who had recently attended college together in Oakland, and a couple of teenager boys.

I chose to follow Newton, Seale, and Eldridge Cleaver. It was my choice and a very sincere one.

I became highly visible as a Panther, as you shall see. I early on made speeches in Hawaii, Japan, Los Angeles, New England. I was then sent to Los Angeles to organize the Panthers there, along with Bunchy Carter.

I was writing, talking about the Panthers constantly. Then, through contacts given me by James Baldwin, I was offered a contract by The Dial Publishig Company to write *Picking Up The Gun*. The Panther leadership told me I couldn't write the book. I was told in no uncertain terms that I would not be allowed to do on my own in a book what I had been doing—writing and talking about the aims and programs of the Black Panther Party—on their instructions since I'd joined the party. When I protested, I was placed under house arrest.

When I went ahead and signed the book deal, the word on the street was that a contract had been put out on my life. As I worked on the book threats were made to my family.

The nightmare was only beginning. Even before I joined the Panthers I had been contacted and warned "for my own benefit" that the leadership of the Black Liberation Movement in the United States was "Communist contolled." The two men who warmed me, interestingly, had both played football with me in school, but at different times. They now belonged to a special division of the FBI that was charged with spying on "subversive" groups such as the Black Panther Party. At the time the Black Panther Party had about five members, officially. Eldridge Cleaver wasn't even a member yet. But they knew he was about to join up.

In the beginning the contacts with these two FBI men were friendly and harmless. They were keeping a close watch on me, I realized later. And at one point I came to realize they knew everything about me; where my mother and father lived, what my brothers and sister did for a living, everything.

It was all very polite but once I broke with the Panthers over the book, they started playing hardball. Their objectective was to cause a breakup of the Panthers from the inside. It would happen. Long after I was party to meetings and discussions inside Panther headquarters, I often knew, sometimes the very next day, what was discussed there. The FBI men would tell me.

Picking Up the Gun was true as far as it went. In 1970 there was only so far I could go. Remember, the Panthers were having a running war with the police in several cities and states, and I knew a great deal more than I could put on paper. The Panther newspaper had named me a traitor and suggested that my killer would become a hero. And my family continued to receive threats.

By the time *Picking Up The Gun* came out I was running scared; more afraid of my "friends" in the FBI than I was of any Panther threat.

They had me by balls and squeezed whenever they felt like it. They squeezed hard and long. They suggested I move back to San Francisco and become a drug dealer; I moved back to San Francisco and became a drug dealer. They yelled "jump" and I asked them "how high?"

I grew tired and wanted out, demanded out. And that was when the real nightmare started...

Out of all the pain that followed I came to the realization that taking to the streets to fight social revolution in this country is like "spitting in the wind; it will fly back into your face."

Earl Anthony

CHAPTER I

1967 and the Call for "Black Power"

I first heard about it on early morning television. It was August 22, 1989 and Huey P. Newton, the co-founder of the Black Panther Party had been shot to death in a drug infested West Oakland, California neighborhood. A few days afterwards, his alleged assailant, Tyrone Robinson, a twenty-five year old member of the notorious prison and narcotics gang, the Black Guerrilla Family, was captured along with two other young black men who were with him that early morning, at approximately 5:15 a.m., when Oakland police say he killed Newton in an argument pertaining to the purchase of crack cocaine.

The stories coming from the media about the killing of Newton talked about his 1960s reputation as a black revolutionary in detail, but more or less overlooked his volatile lifestyle of the 1970s and 1980s in the streets and politics of Oakland.

The funeral for Huey Newton, who along with Bobby G. Seale, founded the infamous Black Panther Party in Oakland in 1966, was held Monday, August 28, 1989 in the same city. The service was attended by a few thousand mourners.

Huey Newton died an enigma. He was idolized by a generation of blacks, Latinos, and radical whites from the 1960s. But on another level in the 1970s and 1980s Newton was to make both friends and enemies because of his personal, political, and business dealings in Oakland.

I first met Huey Newton in February, 1967, when the Black Panther Party was in its infancy. The occasion was a meeting of representivies of all the, what was referred to as "black nationalists" organizations in the Bay Area at the Black House. The Black House was a place frequented by artists, writers, poets, and actors, including Ed Bullins, the playwright, Marvin X Jackson, the poet, and Eldridge Cleaver, ex-convict and best-selling author of *Soul on Ice.*

Actually, I'd had occasion to observe Newton and listen to a speech he'd made at a rally a couple of weeks earlier in Golden Gate Park. But my personal introduction to him came about at the Black House. However, before we get into the purpose of that meeting, allow me to remind you of what had come down in the United States in the mid-1960s and the mood of, primarily young, black nationalists at the time, and especially those of us who lived in the San Francisco-Oakland area.

Following the shooting of a sixteen-year-old black youth named Matthew Johnson in the summer of 1966 by a white policeman in the Hunter's Point housing project, the anger of Bay Area blacks exploded. Young Johnson was killed by the San Francisco policeman for allegedly stealing a car. He was unarmed.

At the time, there was already a strange and ominous mood pervading the black communities across the United States. It was that summer that Stokely Carmichael and SNCC sent out the "Black Power" battle cry. People were, as poet Marvin X Jackmon put it, "sick and tired of being sick and tired."

The murder of young Matthew Johnson was the trigger that set off Bay Area blacks. Following a pattern that had been set by black brothers in Harlem in 1964, in Watts in 1965, and in other black urban areas during that period, black people, in their wrath, broke into the streets. Buildings were torched, stores were looted, and for three or four days warehouses burned in the Hunters Point and Fillmore districts of San Francisco, and sniper fire was exchanged with the police. A few days later, Oakland exploded and the pattern was repeated. For many of us it was an indelible and life-changing experience; a revolutionary breed of black men and women were born.

And so it was, as we progressed toward 1967, a new set of dynamics gave fresh motivation to those of us in the Bay Area who were actively involved in the black liberation movement. People were beginning to group together, to talk about what they could do and make certain efforts to put things in motion. People had finally discovered what it meant to be black in a political connection, and that there was a distinct problem in this country directly related to their skin color. We had to look for new solutions to our problems. As black revolutionary theoretician Frantz Fanon said in his manifesto, *The Wretched of the Earth*: "Violence is a cleansing force. It frees the native from his inferiority complex and from his despair and inaction; it makes him fearless and restores his self-respect." It was this type of chemistry—activated by the revolts in the cities—that was operating on people to whatever degree in the winter of 1966-67.

People I knew and knew about were reading and quoting Fanon. To us he was the apostle of violence. *The Wretched of the Earth* was like a road map to revolution, and if you were honest, and intelligent enough not to misinterpret what you read, you could look on the map and locate the distance you had traveled on the journey. But at the end you knew there was an armed struggle. This was what we were finally talking about, then. But this type of talk was reserved for our most romantic verbal ventures into the hows of solving the problems of black people in the United States.

I had been invited to participate in the planning of the commemoration for Malcolm X, held in Golden Gate Park in early February, because, at the time, I was chairman of the Independent Action Movement (I AM). The organization had existed for nearly a year, and we were mainly involved in leading a rent strike against the San Francisco Public Housing Authority to secure better housing for poor people who were public housing tenants. We were also involved in leading school boycotts in an effort to get more black teachers and so forth. We, like everyone else at the time, had styled ourselves after the SNCC pattern of emphasizing black community organization at every level. Most of us were college students.

I really became aware of the need for better housing when I, as a law student, had gotten a job with the San Francisco Housing Authority. One of my tenants from the Fillmore District, Audrey Smith, was very vocal in her complaints about the Housing Authority and, even though I worked for "the company," I totally agreed with the many complaints, I was getting from Audrey and the other tenants.

After a few discussions, Audrey Smith and I decided to form tenant unions in San Francisco public housing. Our aim was to ask for changes for the betterment of the housing project, including scattered housing, where public housing tenants could live in residential areas, not just in the projects. Within a couple of months, with Earl Williams of Potrero Hill joining us, we had ourselves a union. Of course I was doing this clandestinely because, obviously, I was supposed to be taking care of tenant complaints—which amounted to nothing more than doing patchwork to keep the more vocal ones, like Audrey Smith, from making waves. Our organization started slow, with small meetings.

Of course it was bound to happpen; I got found out by Eneas Kane, the San Francisco Housing Authority Director who was told by a fellow employee that I was organizing the tenants to get better living conditions. I was fired, the reason being that I used a Housing Authority car after working hours. It was a ridiculous charge, for I had a new Pontiac LeMans of my own to drive after working hours.

However, it got me fired, and then twelve black tenants came, with protest signs, to a San Francisco Housing Authority Director's meeting while my case was being heard. The newspapers were also there and the following day the protest of my firing was one of the main stories in the daily papers.

I then went to San Francisco City College, and talked to a Black Student Union meeting. I asked for recruits to help me with the tenant union so we might organize a public housing strike.

Bill Ballon and Joe Ravarra were the first to join me; others quickly followed. Bill Ballon got me in touch with Hank Jones and Chuck Morton in the next couple of days and we had our organization, Independent Action Movement (I AM). We soon gained a great deal of publicity and would become the civil rights group that organized the most successful public housing rent strike in the history of America. After the riots of that summer we had no trouble signing up new workers, or getting all the publicity we wanted. We had become a force in San Francisco. I had, in the meantime, been made director of a government funded anti-poverty program with twenty-five employees working for me. That was the way matters stood with me when I was approached about taking part in the Malcolm X Commemoration.

The person who contacted me was a white woman lawyer named Beverly Axelrod. She had recently gotten a lot of publicity because she had been the mastermind behind Eldridge Cleaver's release from prison, after his serving nine years on a charge of rape, and becoming the best-selling author of *Soul On Ice*. She called and asked me to meet her in a coffee shop near the St. Francis Hotel. I didn't know it yet but she was the front woman for a group of white influential Communists who were planning to promote Eldridge Cleaver as the next Malcolm X.

Cleaver, since getting out of jail, had rented a large Victorian house, which he called the Black House and opened a communal political and cultural center where he held weekly meetings on politics and political affairs, as well as a Saturday night soicals. I would come to learn that Beverly Axelrod and her friends were picking up the tab.

At any rate, I went to meet Beverly Axelrod on the appointed day for coffee, and for her to extend a formal invitation to I AM to take part in the Malcolm X Commemoration.

She had Eldridge Clever with her—she was his mistress, I had been told—and it was the first time I'd ever met either one of them, although I certainly knew who Cleaver was and had observed him at the couple of Black House functions I'd attended.

I accepted the invitation to attend the rally at Golden Gate Park, and she asked me to make a speech on "Urban Problems." She explained that Roy Ballard, the San Francisco SNCC organizer, had organized the conference where plans were to be made both for the honoring of the martyred Black Muslim leader and a protest to the U.S. Congress for the recent ousting of Adam Clayton Powell.

I had never met most of the other young black nationalists leaders who attended the meeting at Golden Gate Park. I had come from Los Angeles, as a graduate of the University of Southern California, to attend law school in San Francisco. From waspy USC, Greek fraternity, membership in the Young Republicans, to Golden Gate College of Law and a quick introduction to radical politics in one rather drastic and quick step.

Up until then I'd not had time to cultivate friendships among the black liberation movement set, as I AM was just too involved in the rent strike. There must have been thirty to forty speakers altogether, on every subject you could think of. Among them were Eldridge Cleaver speaking on prisons; Ron Karenga on black culture; Huey Newton—and we didn't actually talk, this was my introduction to Newton—on politics. Bobby Seale and Roy Ballard were among the others that spoke.

Ballard called on the group to participate in a week long commemoration for Malcolm X, and also for a show of support for Adam Clayton Powell. He was also chasing the elusive dream of uniting the various fractions of black radicals that had come into existence in the Bay Area. There were appearances by Afro and jazz combos, art exhibits and a fashion show put on by the Black Student Union of San Francisco State College.

We got organized, if loosely, that day and not only did we decide to have the commemoration in honor of Malcolm X, but also to protest against the Congress for its harassment of black New York Congressman Adam Clayton Powell, who had just been kicked from his U. S. Congressional seat. It was a volatile time, or to quote the words of Cuban Revolutionary poet, Jose Marti: "It is the time of the furnaces, and it is only necessary to see the glow." We were beginning to see the glow.

The Ad Hoc Committee of young Bay Area Black Nationalists who attended the meeting at Golden Gate Park decided to get together every Friday at the Black House to plan the Malcolm X memorial. It was decided that Betty Shabazz, the widow of Malcolm X, would be the keynote speaker on opening day, and the final event would be a pilgrimage to the death site of Matthew Johnson. For the entire week there would be something going on from 10 a.m. in the morning, until 2 a.m. the next morning.

Then the discussion came up as to how the security of Betty Shabazz would be handled and Roy Ballard suggested that responsibility be turned over to the Black Panther Party for Self-Defense, a new paramilitary organization that was based in Oakland, and had been founded three or so months before by Huey Newton and Bobby Seale.

At that time there were many different Black Panther organizations, taking their names and symbolism from the Lowdnes County (Alabama) Freedom Organization that SNCC had played a major role in organizing, and there were two of these Black Panther organizations in the Bay Area; the Oakland based group, the Black Panther Party for Self-Defense, and the San Francisco group, which was simply called the Black Panther Party. There was much debate around that time about the factors that distinguished one from the other. The San Francisco organization, which was headed by Ken Freeman, said that it was political whereas the Oakland group was military (the San Francisco group was to fold shortly after the Malcolm X Commemoration, pressured, it is my belief, by the FBI). Huey Newton and Bobby Seale, however, said they were both political and military. And when the San Francisco group folded they took the name, the Black Panther Party, or BPP as it came to be called in newspaper headlines around the world.

At the time of that meeting in Golden Gate Park, however, it was all somewhat beside the point. Not many people outside the black community of Oakland had heard of Huey Newton, Bobby Seale, and their group—and, to tell the truth, they just about were their group at the time. They could call up maybe a dozen men to participate in activities but there were only a five hardcore members. All that changed, however, on February 21, 1967.

CHAPTER II

Huey Newton and the Black Panthers

The Malcolm X Commemoration was to be financed by chapters of white San Francisco Communist Party members, and while most of those participating in honoring Malcolm X were ignorant of that fact, I was not. I had been contacted by two old "friends" by the names of Ron Kizenski and Robert O'Connor and briefed as to what was coming down politically. In that area, I later realized, I was somewhat naive and terribly confused. After all, I was a law student, a graduate of the University of Southern California, from a black middle class background and very idealistic. I saw poverty and unfairness all around me, yet I had been raised to a great extent to believe in the system—The American Way. And that is exactly why I was taking time away from my law studies and putting myself in the street in an attempt to do something about what I saw as an unfair situation. Wasn't that the American Way I'd been taught to believe in?

And that is exactly why I was contacted by the two men from the COINTELPRO Unit of the Federal Bureau of Investigation, O'Connor and Kizenski, both of whom had been known to me through past school activities, but certainly not as agents of the FBI.

As it turned out, not many people outside of Oakland had ever heard of Huey Newton and the Black Panther Party for

Self-Defense. But COINTELPRO certainly had. However, when they contacted me, shortly after Beverly Axelrod invited me to speak at the Golden Gate Park rally, they were much more interested in Axelrod and Eldridge Cleaver than they were in a small group of Oakland black men who were wearing berets and carrying pistols. That was a matter for the local police. Nevertheless, COINTELPRO was interested in all black liberation groups, as it would turn out.

They saw me as a black "Young Republican" from USC who'd observed a social situation out there in the streets of San Francisco that needed changing and, with total sincerity, I was out there as a law student, trying to change it. I was not asked to "spy" on the black nationalists organizations at that first meeting nor was I even asked to report back to anyone.

The tone of the conversation was sort of like: "well, we know you and we know your background and it is a fine thing you're trying to do, attempting to get these poor people better housing. But we're all friends here and we're just telling you to keep your eyes open. Some of these people you're dealing with are Communists and this meeting where you've been invited to speak is backed with Communist money. So, just be careful. You're an young Negro of impeccable background, just the sort of person these Commies go after. That's why Beverly Axelrod contacted you, you know. You're just the type of person they're after. Don't let them dupe you. We have your best interest at heart." Sure, they did. They also already had their hooks in me, but I didn't know that yet.

It was agreed at the Golden Gate Park meeting that we would have a special conference at the Black House to meet with Newton and Seale about security. The meeting was scheduled for the following Friday.

I took a few members of I AM with me and we arrived late. As we walked in, I immediately noticed two young brothers in the far and near corners of the north side of the room, standing at military "at ease" with carbines resting snugly in their arms. There must have been about twenty to thirty people at the meeting and they were seated in a circle. Many of the faces were familiar ones in the local black nationalist set; among them Barbara Arthur, Roy Ballard, Mark Comfort. At the south side of the room was Eldridge Cleaver, who was chairing the meeting. Opposite Cleaver, on the north side of the room, sat Bobby Seale, Huey Newton, and another of their aides, Little Bobby Hutton. Bobby Hutton would become the first Black Panther to be killed by the police, in a shootout after Martin Luther King was assassinated in Memphis, Tennessee on April 6, 1968. Little Bobby and I were also to become good friends. The other aides, standing as guards, were Reggie and Sherman Fortier. They were all dressed in black, with Huey holding a shotgun, and Bobby with a .45 strapped to his side. Huey and Bobby seemed aloof from everybody else, but serious and determined. The effect was high drama.

This meeting was different in some important ways from any black nationalist meetings I had previously attended, and I had attended many in the last year. For one thing, there was none of that circuitous debate over each matter brought to the floor, which had become standard. When Cleaver (who was not yet a member of the Black Panthers, although he definitely played off the Panthers' image that night) put a motion on the floor that the group adopt the BPPSD's Ten Point Program, there was not a word of dissent. This was so unusual for this group that Cleaver commented, rather facetiously, "I know somebody must have something to say?" Another thing which was so different at that meeting was the feeling of revolutionary discipline and commitment. Nobody budged when Cleaver asked anyone who was not serious to leave. I don't believe everyone was serious, or at least serious about that meeting, but I also know that nobody wanted all eyes riveted on him—or her—while doing a long walk to the front door.

Huey, Bobby and the brothers with guns really made a difference that night. The whole scene blew my mind. I wanted to find out everything I could about the Black Panther Party for Self-Defense, and about Eldridge Cleaver. By this time it was easy to get information. People in the black nationalist movement had started to nit-pick. They were begining to complain about the aloofness of Huey, Bobby and their men at the Saturday night social parties. They bitched that the BPPSD was not political. As for Cleaver, they dismissed him out-of-hand because he was in love with a white woman who was said to be a Communist. The more I heard the more convinced I became that Cleaver and BPPSD had to be all right because this particular group of Black House regulars only criticized people who were actually doing something, and thereby leaving them behind.

Later on that night, I asked a close friend of mine, Bill Ballon, to tell me more about the Black Panther Party for Self-Defense.

Bill related to me what he knew—how Huey Newton had enlisted Bobby Seale to found the organization, the Black Panther Party for Self-Defense, with him because Newton, himself, believed that black people had to be armed, to have a type of military power, because they were powerless in other ways. He told me that Huey and Bobby had hooked up with each other at Merritt College, where both were members of the Soul Students Advisory Council, and that they had armed a few young blacks in Oakland. They patrolled the Oakland streets at night, looking for police abuse of blacks; and if they saw a policeman with a black suspect, Newton would get out of the car with a law book and armed with a sawed-off shotgun and explain the black suspect his legal rights.

At the special meeting to talk about Betty Shabazz's security, I was first formally introduced to Huey Newton. He wore the uniform of the Black Panther Party, as it was to become known—the black beret cocked to the side of his coiffred Afro; the black leather jacket; black pants, black shoes and socks; and white shirt. He was about five feet nine inches tall, light complexion, with chiseled features, and a tenor voice. Many women have commented to me how exceedingly handsome they found Huey Newton; in fact, when he was in jail during the 1960s, the Black Panther Party had a saying: "If you so much as touch a hair on Huey's pretty head, you better give your soul to the Lord because your ass belongs to the Black Panther Party."

The first time I saw Huey in action was on February 21, 1967, when about twenty of us, armed with shotguns, pistols, and carbines, went into a car cordon to the San Francisco Airport—led by Newton. We picked up Betty Shabazz, and, followed by the San Francisco police who had us under-surveillance, we traveled to the North Beach area of the city so that Betty might have an interview at *Ramparts* Magazine with Eldridge Cleaver.

When we were about to leave after Betty Shabazz's interview, there were at least a hundred San Fransisco police around us. One of the cops, a rotund red-faced man rushed our position, his gun drawn—and Huey moved toward him cocking his sawed-off shotgun, and threatened the policeman. The policeman backed down. Eldridge Cleaver called it, "The Courage to Kill," when he described the incident in an article about Newton in *Ramparts*.

I was so impressed with Huey Newton that day, when he confronted that policeman in North Beach, that I decided to join the Panthers. At this point I was most impressed with not only Huey Newton and Bobby Seale, but also with Eldridge Cleaver in spite of some misgivings about the "Communist Connection." Also, some renegade Black Muslims with whom I'd been sharing an apartment since shortly after I arrived in San Francisco expressed doubts about Eldridge who had joined the Black Muslims himself while in prison. They warned me that "white folks" were using Cleaver to make a fool of black people, by having him talk about "taking up arms" against the American government; and they were finally proven right. Eventually, over 300 black men were to be killed by the Cleaver led Black Panther Party; more than ninety-five percent of them by fellow Black Panthers who accused each other of being FBI or police informers. These were all internal killings.

Although I talked with Cleaver and spoke about joining the BPP, before that could happen, I had to go to Los Angeles for a conference being given by black cultural nationalist, Ron Karenga. I had accepted the invitation to attend some time before and while Karenga was in San Francisco for the Malcolm X Conference, he had reminded me that I was to attend and make a speech. He'd also invited several other black nationalist leaders to come down for his conference while he as in San Francisco but not Cleaver or Bobby Seale and Huey Newton.

Six carloads of us young San Francisco black activists drove to Los Angeles a week later for Ron Karenga's US black cultural conference. The speakers included Karenga, of course, and Stokely Carmichael. I spoke on the public housing strike, which was now a success; all of our demands had been met.

When I got back to San Francisco, I arranged a meeting between Eldridge Cleaver, myself as chairman of I AM, and Bill Ballon and Hank Jones and Chuck Morton as well as other members of I AM. We met at my office on Portreo Hill. I wanted us all to go Black Panther with Cleaver. They refused to follow me because they disliked the fact that Eldridge Cleaver was totally supported and advised by white Communists.

I quit as Chairman of the Independent Action Movement, and became the eighth member to join the Black Panther Party.

Cleaver set up a meeting for me with Bobby Seale at the home of Beverly Axelrod. Upon his release she had gotten him his position with *Ramparts* magazine and then, at a party she threw for him, introduced him to the leaders of the San Francisco black nationalist set. Some of these same people were now attacking Cleaver for his affilation with her, not because of her political bent so much as because she was white.

Bobby Seale, a tall, slender, brown skinned man, answered the doorbell. He was in shirt sleeves with a .45 caliber pistol tucked into his pants. Seale didn't know me and was very abrupt and businesslike (later I was to learn that was just the way he was). He told me that Eldridge wasn't in and I should try back again later that afternoon.

When I returned later, Cleaver was there. He introduced me to five or six Panthers—the entire membership with the exception of Huey Newton, who was nowhere about. Then the two of us went into another room and talked. He seemed interested in my desire to join the Panthers but cautious. Up until that point all the membership, with the exception of Eldridge, were home boys from the Oakland area. On the other hand, I had worked on the planning committee of the Malcolm X memorial with people who were highly critical of Cleaver in particular and the Black Panther Party of Oakland in general. Eldridge knew that I'd stayed away from personally criticizing either him or the BPP.

He told me that he'd read a position paper on the San Francisco public rent strike that I had done for the Hunters Point community paper, *The Spokesman*, and he thought my political thinking was sound. He asked what year I was in in law school. I told him I was in my final year.

"Good," he said and pondered that bit of information in silence as if quickly fitting that piece of information into some sort of master plan he seemed to have in his mind.

"We're going to need black lawyers in the liberation movement," he said.

Then he went on to explain that he had altered his political direction; that he was no longer trying to form an umbrella organization over the various black nationalists groups in the area doing their separate thing as he'd been trying to do at the Black House. I sensed that he must have been very disappointed with the futility of his efforts. My own experience with the various organizations of the Bay Area had driven home the message that we were far from reaching the point where we realized the necessity of joint action. Cleaver explained that from now on he was dedicating himself to the Black Panther Party, and to building armed defense units in black communities across the country. He told me that he'd walked the streets with Huey Newton and Bobby Seale, and that they were doing the best job of organizing he had seen.

I agreed with him. What I didn't realize at the time was that Cleaver had taken the Black Panther Party off the "streets" in a way, and into the home of Beverly Axelrod. She and her white radical friends would become increasingly more influential in BPP policy and activity.

I was then taken to talk with Bobby Seale, Chairman of the Party, who would make the decision as to whether I would be accepted. I was, and I joined the Black Panther Party, the eighth member to actually sign up officially. My two friends who'd come calling wearing three piece suits and shoulder arms to warn me about the "Commie influence" in the black nationalist movement were, I'd learn later, pleased. With the Black Panther Party now within a Communist sphere of influence, and what they were already thinking of as their "boy" in the Party, they realized they couldn't have planned it better if they'd tried. I've never really been sure they didn't plan it.

My first Black Panther assignment was to organize a rally in the Potrero Hill section of town where I was a consultant for a federal government anti-poverty program. By then, the spring of 1967, the Economic Opportunity Council, or anti-poverty programs, supported by the federal government, were in progress. It was part of President Lyndon Baines Johnson's "Great Society" programs—aimed at settling unrest, riots, and demonstrations in the black community.

However, in San Francisco, black civil rights activits used the federal programs, and their money, to finance exactly the sort of activity the programs were set up to stop. I'd gotten together with Earl Williams and Walter Robinson and we decided to write proposals to get anti-poverty money for the Potrero Hill section of San Francisco.

I wrote the proposal, and we submitted it to the downtown San Francisco office, to submit to Washington. It was for five million dollars for two years, to start up a community employment agency.

The money was granted to us, and in that spring of 1967, I became consultant for our newly formed organization, the Potrero Hill Manpower Program.

I had members of I AM, who got jobs with Potrero Hill Manpower, to scour the area with leaflets asking people to come to our meetings, to see about getting jobs as job recruiters.

At our first meeting we set about electing a Board of Directors, and deciding as to who would get the eighteen jobs alotted as recruiters.

Unfortunately, we had to shelve that plan, because that first night, when we asked for nominations for the jobs, several fist fights broke out, which Chuck Morton, as enforcer, had to break up by firing his pistol. (In 1969, Chuck, who was hot tempered, was killed by the police, after going berserk and killing six innocent white people on a bus.)

I was getting twenty-thousand dollars a year, for ten hours a week work. That was good money in 1967. As a matter of fact, most of the budget was going to the twenty-five employees of Potrero Hill Manpower and the money was almost equal for everyone. One of the big problems with the anti-poverty programs across America—and it was well known at the time—was that almost all the money went to pay the salary of a few anti-poverty workers.

The whole thing became something of a trip. I would have to put up with domestic problems, which caused prolonged absences from work on part of the women, and most of the men refused to come to work. They just sat on the corner drinking wine. And I couldn't fire them because they'd become friends with the other public rent strike organizers. I organized two major job fairs in the Potrero Hill section but less than a hundred public housing tenants from the area showed up for each one because the Manpower project employees refused to solicit people to come by or hand out our leaflets urging them to come. The women who worked for us continued to stay home, the men continuted to drink wine on the corner, and they all received paychecks because they refused to be fired. I became extremely disappointed in the anti-poverty program.

And this was the way things stood when I organized the Potrero Hill rally for the Black Panthers. However, word of the Panthers had gotten around; Huey and Bobby spoke to hundreds of blacks in the public housing project.

After the early morning rally, Huey Newton told me he would ride down to Richmond, California with me for another rally we were having for a young black named Denzil Dowell who had been killed by the police. I had a brand new 1967 Pontiac LeMans at the time, and when Huey climbed into the front seat, he complimented me on the car. As Huey and I drove down to Richmond, I got to know him one on one for the first time.

On the way there, Huey briefed me on the facts in the Dowell case. Denzil Dowell was twenty-two years old when he was shot to death on April 1 by a white cop from the Contra Costa sheriff's department. Mark Comfort, a black organizer from Oakland who knew the Dowell family, had asked the Black Panther Party to come down and look into the situation. The Panthers went into Richmond and conducted their own investigation, turning up some interesting things—one of the most interesting of which was that a doctor who had worked on the case told the Dowell family that Denzil had been shot with his hands raised. He had deduced this from the way the bullets had entered the body. Also it became known that Dowell had no gun. Everything pointed to a clear case of unjustifiable homicide.

The Panthers had taken this information directly to the Richmond district attorney and the following day had a meeting with the sheriff of Contra Costa County. At both meetings, which were attended by black people in Richmond, they were armed, and although the agencies of law enforcement were seemingly rigid in their position on the murder, the Party was accomplishing its purpose—the black community was becoming very interested and involved in the Panther investigation.

People came to the Denzil Dowell rally. Black people, old and young. Not just the college students, or the middle class, but the very people who were catching hell every day in that North Richmond community. There were several-hundred people there, gathered in the yard of Denzil's brother's house. Some sat on the lawn, others stood around or milled about. Standing tall and armed were the Black Panthers. There weren't yet too many of us but sometimes, in those days, "soldiers" were recruited to wear the uniform and make a show of force.

As they had done earlier in Potrero Hill, Huey Newton and Bobby Seale talked to the people. They stood on top of a car, and explained the Panthers' Ten Point Program, and why black people should arm themselves, and how they could put an end to wanton murders in the black community such as that of Denzil Dowell. At one point, Huey, explaining the type of weapons black people should get—pointed to the gun in the hands of a Panther brother on the roof of the house behind him. The brother, a Panther named John Sloan, went through a demonstration with his weapon; the people cheered.

The people there in North Richmond that day liked everything they saw about the Panthers. They liked the way Huey and Bobby brashly defied the police—who watched the rally from a safe distance outside the perimeter of the crowd—and the way they openly brandished their weapons. You could see that the Panthers were establishing a relationship to these people on a very fundamental level. It was the police who had killed Dowell, and who daily intimidated black people in North Richmond, as they did in black communities across the country. And it was the policeman's gun at his side that gave him the ultimate power; the power to take someone's life. And here, before their eyes, the people were watching the Panthers shatter the myth of the omnipotence of the police. They were being shown what they always knew in their hearts but had never permitted themselves to admit: The police were just men, but men with guns and the law to back them up. They were being told that to counteract this, black people needed to arm themselves, and then find a way of dealing with the police without getting hung up in legal entanglements.

The Panthers were speaking the language of the people, and the people were listening and understanding. When the Panthers stood there and called on the people of North Richmond, California, to "pick up the gun" those people understood.

Huey and I discussed the events of the day on the way back to San Francisco that night. I really don't know what I'd been expecting but I was elated at the way things had turned out. I had been involved with the Watts insurrection in 1965, and was in the San Francisco revolt of 1966, but I had never seen black men command the respect of the people the way Huey Newton and Bobby Seale did that day.

At a later stage in my development as a member of the Panthers I began to realize that what seemed to me so fantastic was simply a forward step in ideology and tactics in the continuous process of changing the political, social and economic order of America. But what captured my imagination during my early days in the Party, was not only the fact that the Panthers had taken a step forward in ideology and tactics, but the boldness of the style with which that step was taken.

On our way back that night, Huey used an analogy with the unpopular war we were fighting in Vietnam at the time to explain his focus of activities of the Black Panther Party against the police. "The police in America," he said, "are like the Marines in Vietnam. They are in the ghetto to protect the interests of the multinational corporations, and the military/industrial complex that dominates people of color and poor people in America—and around the world."

And Newton was to expand on that theory when he spoke in the streets on behalf of the Panthers, time and time again.

Newton said: "The ultimate goal of the Black Panther Party is to organize for armed revolution in America." He felt a political solution would not work without military force. And, eventually, he wanted to make America an industrial Communist state. That evening was the first time I'd heard him use the word "Communist" and I must admit I found it disturbing. I had not yet come around to his (or Eldridge Cleaver's) way of thinking on Socialism. And when I did, as you shall see, my "conversion" didn't take for very long.

I'd been raised with family and friends who totally believed in the "Evil Empire" of the Soviets. I'd very recently been warned by two men from my past, from school days, now FBI agents, that the entire black liberation front in the Bay Area had been "infiltrated" by Communists; it was fairly well known that Beverly Axelrod was somewhat to the far radical left politically and it was whispered (shouted, in some quarters) among black nationalists that she was the conduit by which the Communists were feeding money in the Bay Area black movement. It was beginning to look very much as if, with Eldridge Cleaver's joining the Panthers, Axelrod and her group had a very real entry into the the black liberation movement. Now Newton was talking the "Communist" line instead of the "Socialism," I'd heard him mention in his public speeches.

I was impressed with Huey's theories on revolution and after the rally in Richmond, I was to see the other side of the complex Newton, the revolutionary theorist; the worldly decadent black street brother.

Newton asked me to stop by a bar in Oakland and have a drink. Newton drank Cuba Libres then; later in in life he was to change his drink to expensive cognac. I drank Scotch.

At the bar, everybody seemed to know him. Newton was a regular. He told me that in the coming week we were going to put together the first Black Panther Party newspaper, thanks to the money contributed to the Panthers from the white Communists, organized as a financial support group, and put together by Beverly Axelrod.

Newton had courage, smarts, and street talent, and was fun to be with, as I was to find out in the next couple of months, as Newton, Seale, Cleaver, a young black graphic artist named Emory Douglas, and I would work all night at Cleaver's apartment in San Francisco writing and designing the weekly Black Panther Party Newspaper—and distributing it. We all became good friends.

That evening at the bar in Oakland, I got some speed pills from Huey that were to keep me up all night. We also smoked some good marijuana. Newton was already heavily into drugs back then, in 1967 (when he was twenty-five years old).

Newton was also heavily into women. That night when I took him to his apartment in Oakland from the bar, he told me he had two young black women coming by later on for a freak set.

The next day which was Sunday, April 30, 1967, the San Francisco *Examiner* came out with a front page headline: "Oakland's Black Panthers Wear Guns, Talk Revolution." It carried a picture of Bobby Seale with a .45 caliber pistol strapped across his shoulder, and Huey Newton with a bandolier of bullets across his chest, and a riot shotgun in his hand. The newspaper story detailed some of the more notorious actions of the Party, including the armed rally and investigation of the death of black youth, Denzil Dowell, in Richmond, and the armed escort provided to Betty Shabazz enroute to her husband's memorial. It also talked about impending gun legislation, which was pending before the California State Legislature in Sacramento.

The day the story broke in the *Examiner*, I was with LeRoi Jones (Imamu Amiri Baraka) and five or six black nationalist activists. After reading the story, Jones mused over it for a minute, stroking the growth of hair under his chin. "It could be dangerous. They usually try to set you up in this way," he said.

This proposed legislation was a thinly disguised attempt to disarm Huey Newton and the Black Panther Party. A few weeks before, Don Mulford, an assemblyman from the Oakland District, had introduced a bill to change the state laws that permitted private citizens to carry loaded weapons as long as they were not concealed. This bill would require permits for such handguns, but not for rifles or shotguns. The law, which Huey Newton had studied, was the foundation upon which the Black Panther Party was built—and Oakland police were strongly suspected of instigating the bill to change it so that they could arrest members of the Party.

On Tuesday, May 2, 1967, I had to answer a subpoena to testify at hearings of the United States Civil Rights Commission in San Francisco. It was about my activities as the leader of the San Francisco rent strike. On the same day, Huey Newton had dispatched a contingent of twenty-four black brothers and six sisters to go to the California State Legislature in Sacramento where the subject of gun legislation was due on the floor and Mulford was scheduled to speak. Huey did not go, because of parole restrictions, and Cleaver only went as a reporter for *Ramparts*. Bobby Seale led that delegation. Seale was to read a message to the media and legislature about the necessity for black people to be armed. It received nationwide headlines, and radio and television coverage. It made new Panthers feel the sort of pride Newton was no doubt thinking about when he said to me later that week: "The only way I'm gonna leave the Party will be in a pine box." He felt that each and every person who joined the Panthers should feel as strongly.

The news media reports out of Sacramento that day caused a national sensation—and, I've been told, sent chills up the backs of many white Americans. Here was a group of heavily armed black men and women.

While the newspaper reports caused excitement among blacks, and especially young black men, it determined the resolve of law enforcement officers all over the country and especially in California. Bobby Seale and several others were arrested immediately, jailed and charged with a variety of crimes.

By 1969, the Black Panther Party would have over 5,000 members. Of this number, more than 3,000 would go to prison when the police and FBI clamped down on the BPP. Over three-hundred others were suspected of being police informants and killed by the Panthers themselves. Another twenty-nine were killed by the police; three in the warfare between the Panthers and Karenga's US group, and still another six were killed in 1971, in the struggle between the Newton and Cleaver factions for control of the group.

Chapter III

Eldridge Cleaver Takes Over the Panthers

Because I'd dropped out of law school and was now a member of the Black Panther Party, my draft board in Los Angeles was trying to reclassify my draft status and put me in the Armed Forces.

And that led me to my first contact with the police as a Panther. It was July 7, 1967. Particularly then, the contacts between blacks and the police were usually abrasive and hostile. That day I was almost into Los Angeles. Little Bobby Hutton and Reggie Fortier were with me. They had been involved in a fight a couple of days before, along with Huey and Bobby Seale, with some members of the American Nazi Party, and it was decided that since I was going to Los Angeles for a week or so, it would be cool for them to go with me and get out of the Bay Area.

The motorcycle cop flashed his bike light on us and signaled for us to pull off the freeway. It was not the best of times for a gabfest with a cop because we were smoking a joint. When we pulled off the freeway, I quickly got out and went back to where the cop was. He was white of course. Did you ever wonder why so few motorcycle cops are black? I was stalling for time while Reggie was supposedly getting rid of the marijuana.

After searching me for weapons, the cop ordered me to open

the trunk of the Le Mans. Then he took a look at the stack of Black Panther newspapers and I thought he was going to have a stroke. He became tense and estatically excited. He closed the trunk, ordered me to put my hands, extended, on the trunk of the car, then unhooked the strap on his holster, pulled his service revolver and cocked the hammer.

He ordered Bobby and Reggie out of the car. They hesitated for what seemed like an eternity to me—because I knew this cop was so excited that I figured he was liable to do something foolish—like shoot us all. A newspaper headline flashed before my eyes: "POLICEMAN KILLS THREE BLACK PANTHERS IN SELF DEFENSE!"

Finally, Bobby climbed out of the back seat and, following the order of the cop, put his hands on the top of the car. Reggie still remained inside. The cop ordered Reggie to get out twice more, and was obviously getting nervous. Finally Reggie got out of the car. I saw what was taking him so long; he was still holding the package that had three joints in it in his hand. I asked him later, in jail, why he hadn't just eaten them and he replied that he figured we'd need them with the weekend upon us!

The cop didn't see Reggie drop the package on the ground but noticed when he accidentially stepped on it. He really got excited then and got on his radio, covering us all the while with his pistol, and started shouting about Black Panthers and marijuana cigarettes. Five minutes later there were cops all over the place, ten of them in all. They hauled us off and booked us but cut Little Bobby loose after questioning. The police do that, hoping to arouse suspicion in the other crime partners that the one let go had "talked." Reggie and I knew better. Little Bobby was the first brother recruited by Huey and Bobby Seale into the Party. He was only sixteen and had worked the summer of 1966 on a poverty program job where Bobby Seale had been his counselor. Little Bobby was the treasurer of the Party. The police kept asking Reggie and me about the Black Panther Party. They had confiscated the newspapers and, while we were sitting around waiting to be taken to jail, read them aloud to each other and laughed. They seemed to get a big kick out of the paper—and capturing "dangerous Black Panthers." We were jailed and released on bail. We later beat the case because of illegal search and seizure.

Later that week, I appeared before my draft status review board in Van Nuys, California. I wore a black leather jacket and black denim pants, the trademark of the Black Panther Party, and appeared before five middle aged white men. The first thing they asked was what, exactly, was I doing now that I was no longer in law school.

I pulled typewritten prepared statements from my attache case which I had brought with me, and which I read to the draft board: "To the imperialist, war mongering draft board of Earl Leon Anthony, also known in the Black Muslims as Earl 37X, and in the Black Panther Party as Captain Earl Anthony, the eighth member to join the Black Panther Party . . ." As I read, there was silence.

"I refuse to go into the Armed Forces, so that you might send me to Southeast Asia to fight the yellow man, the Vietnamese, who is not my enemy—but my friend. He is a Communist, the North Vietnamese. I am a Communist, and a black American, and member of the Armed Revolutionary Black Panther Party. We both want to destroy capitalism, and the bastion of capitalism, the American military/industrial complex." I continued to read to the draft board. They now wore worried expressions.

"If I was to be drafted anyway, I would go into the Army, and try to organize fellow blacks and whites, for the Black Panther Party does not believe in racism, to try to flee the country, and go to Cuba—and become examples to those who have refused to become puppets in America's efforts to make the North Vietnamese slaves.

"If they do send me to Vietnam, I will shoot my lieutenant and sergeant in the head once we get into the field, and escape over to the North Vietnamese. So I am telling the draft board . . .Hell no, I won't go. Draft me at your own risk."

After I got finished, I passed out copies of this prepared statement to the members of the draft board. They quickly dismissed me, with no further questions.

A couple of weeks later, near the end of August, I was paid a surprise visited to my San Francisco apartment by Robert O'Connor and Ron Kizenski. No longer were we playing by the "buddy buddy" rules. They were all business this time. They came right to the point: I was under investigation for the bombing of my Van Nuys draft board. I was stunned. Not only did I know nothing about the bombing, I hadn't even been told or heard on the news that the place had been bombed.

Of course they said they didn't believe me, but would offer me a deal. They would not charge me if I would become an informant for the FBI inside the Black Panther Party. I started laughing, and instantly O'Connor threw a right fist upside my jaw, knocking me against the wall. Kizenski grabbed me, and O'Connor threw a series of rights and lefts, knocking me unconscious.

When I regained consciousness, they were still there, sitting down with guns drawn on me. Kizenski said something about them being Vietnam vets and that they didn't like my "smartass" attitude. They proposed their deal to me again. They would get the charges of bombing my draft board dropped, because no one was killed, if I became an FBI informant-agent-provocateur inside the Black Panther Party.

I agreed and as far as I know, became the first of dozens of Black Panthers who were to accept the same type of deal from the FBI's COINTELPRO division. Still others became local police informants. There were soon so many of us that we were informing on each other.

Kizenski and O'Connor said they were transferring from Washington, D.C., to San Francisco; to surveillance of the Black Panther Party, and we were to meet at the beach, along Pacific Coast Highway, at four in the morning each Tuesday. If I missed a Tuesday, they would know it was impossible for me to get there, and they could contact me the next morning, and each suceeding morning until they got in touch with me. At this meetings we were to discuss our strategy for the week.

Within the next few days I was invited to Providence, Rhode Island to speak before a group of blacks who were interested in boycotting the Board of Education because of abuse to black students. A friend of mine in Providence had told of my efforts in San Francisco boycotting the Board of Education while leading I AM.

Things were slow with the Black Panther Party at the moment. Huey Newton, Eldridge Cleaver, Emory Douglas, and I were working on putting out our weekly Black Panther newspaper, which, of course, was financed and distributed by the American Communist movement.

Meanwhile, with Bobby Seale in jail, serving time for his part in the "armed demonstration" at California State Legislature back in May, some of the spark was missing. It was during this time that I came to realize just how much Bobby brought to the Panthers, and that he contributed a great more in leadership qualities than had been apparent, even to those of us close to the situation.

Seale was consulted and it was decided by the leadership of the Panthers—Newton, Cleaver, and Seale, of course—that my traveling and spreading the word about the Black Panthers was a good idea. They approved my trip to Providence, Rhode Island—and so did my FBI "shadows," Kizenski and O'Connor.

In early September, I traveled to Providence, where I spoke to rallies, and on radio. I was also interviewed by the newspaper. As it turned out, all of this activity was reported at length in my FBI files. Interestingly, the regular FBI was trying all along to figure out what I was doing traveling back east. In a frenzy of alarm, they notified: (1) The Rhode Island State Police; (2) The Special Agent in Charge, United States Secret Service, Providence; (3) The United States Army; (4) The United States Naval Base at Newport, Rhode Island; and (5) The Air Force Office of Special Investigations at

Davisville, Rhode Island. And one of the interviews I gave was conducted by an FBI agent pretending to be from the media, who reported back that I was "engaged in inflammatory speeches and is attempting to recruit Negroes into the Black Panther movement." And so I was. But aren't you glad to know your tax dollars were working so well for you in 1967.

They finally decided that I was doing nothing more or less than plotting revolution with other black national "extremists." From Providence I traveled to Boston to meet with organizers of SNCC and then on to New York to meet with other "extremists." Of course we were plotting revolution but COINTELPRO knew exactly what we were doing; they just weren't letting their less exotic FBI brothers know what was going down and how much about it they knew.

Back in San Francisco, it was obvious that the Party was at a low ebb. Part of the reason was that Bobby was still in jail, and the police harrassed us every time we hit the streets. Eldridge, however, wouldn't allow us to get too depressed over the fact that so many of our friends had been arrested since the May demonstration in Sacramento. He kept the faith. He said to me one night: "The Party is going to take over California in 1968." I believed him at the moment.

The night of October 26 was the last time I was to see Huey as a free man for several years. We had stopped by Eldridge's apartment and the four of us (Kathleen was included) were talking about a variety of subjects. The one I remember, that stands out in my mind, was a discussion of Thomas Wolfe's *Look Homeward Angel.* Huey was discussng the significance of a passage where Wolfe talks about crossing the river and getting to the other side, and never being able to go back. He saw a parallel in making a commitment to fight for your liberation as a black man and never being able to submit again.

Later, Huey and I went over to a place where James Baldwin was staying at the time and gave him some Black Panther newspapers and chatted with him for a while. Then we went across the Bay to Oakland and stopped at a few clubs. Eventually Huey brought me back to San Francisco, and left me at the Half Note, a night club on Divisadero Street in San Francisco. I watched him walk out the door. It was to be the last time I was to see him free for a very long time.

It was about four in the morning of October 28, 1967, that I heard the newscast on a soul music station: Black Panther founder Huey P. Newton had been seriously wounded in an early morning gun battle with two policemen. One, a John Frey, was dead. The other policeman, Herbert Heanes, was seriously wounded. Huey was taken to Kaiser Hospital in Oakland. Then they charged him with first degree murder, and he was sent to the hospital ward of San Quentin Prison a few days later. The news we were getting was that he lay close to death.

During that period I was mentally paralyzed with shock. I blamed the Oakland police, of course, and in *Picking Up The Gun*, I cursed the "lousy Oakland police, for I knew that they were down wrong, and had tried to set up brother Huey." I'd later learn that was not exactly what happened.

With Seale in jail, and Huey Newton now in a jail hospital, Cleaver took charge of the Panthers. Two days after Huey's shooting, I went down to Los Angeles for a few days—and to get away as Oakland had become depressing and Kizenski and O'Connor had also called on me to find out "what I knew" about Huey's shootout with the police. When I got back I immediately called on Eldridge.

Cleaver filled me in on the rally that had been held for Newton in Hunters Point a couple of days before, and how two housing authority policemen had been shot to death, which I was already aware of as the Los Angeles papers made a big deal out of it. He did not know who had done the shooting but was absolutely certain that no one connected with the Panthers had anything to do with it.

Clever felt that the Newton shooting could be used as an organizing tool to spread revolution in this country, and that a Free Huey Newton campaign, which the white Communists and radicals were suggesting to Cleaver and myself in meetings we held with them during those early weeks after the Newton shootout, would be the vehicle to make the Black Panther Party the vanguard in a revolutionary movement in America.

Eldridge Cleaver was now running the Black Panther Party but he wasn't alone. One night back in the summer, he'd asked me to go to San Francisco International airport with him. He told me he was going to pick up his "righteous woman," who was coming in from Nashville, Tennessee. The woman we picked up was tall, slender, light of complexion, and wore her red hair in a big Afro. With her were two men, a Caucasion whose name I never could recall, and Fred Brooks, a heavy set brother who was then Director of the Nashville office of SNCC. Kathleen had been working with SNCC as a program secretary in the campus operations. It was she whom Eldridge referred to as his "righteous woman."

Brooks and the Caucasion man only stayed a few days but Kathleen Neal had come to the Bay Area to live and she quickly became an integral part of the BPP operation. Eldridge had met her back in the spring at a student conference held at Fisk University in Nashville, when he was there to write a *Ramparts* story on Stokely Carmichael. She would later marry Eldridge and become known to the political aware world as Kathleen Cleaver.

On November 13, 1967 the Alemeda County Grand Jury returned a three-count indictment against Huey: murder, assault with a deadly weapon on a police officer, and kidnapping. By the time of the indictment he had been transferred from the hospital ward at San Quentin Prison to a single cell on the tenth floor of the Alameda County Courthouse in Oakland. Visiting hours were 1:00 p.m. to 3:00 p.m., three times a week.

I visited Huey was the first visiting day. The little hallway leading into the larger visiting room was jammed full of Panthers and friends of Huey. When I talked to him, his morale was high, and I remember him telling me that when he was in Kaiser with the bullet wound to the stomach, he kept saying to himself: "I'm too mean to die; I'm too mean to die." It was vintage, tough-guy Newton.

I constantly reported to my FBI shadows, Kizenski and O'Connor, and their feeling was that the Black Panther Party would die, if we cut off their support from the white Communists and radicals. And even though they knew I didn't know anything about the Hunters Point shooting of the two housing authority police, they said they would bring me in on conspiracy to murder, because I had led the rent strike in Hunters Point, and was a Black Panther, if I failed to cooperate with them. They also pointed out that the statute of limitations for murder never expired. I knew the FBI had me hooked, even though I begged to get out now that Huey Newton, the leader of the Panthers, was going to be charged with murder and they also had Bobby Seale in jail.

Kizenski and O'Connor were unrelenting. I could not get out because the black extremist and white Communist/radical movement were hand-in-hand and were spreading throughout the nation.

Their plan of action was for me to hype up Cleaver and get him to go into warfare against other black nationalists who had been protesting in front of *Ramparts* magazine against the Black Panther Party because it was supported financially and ideologically by the Communist Party of America.

I began to express the FBI tactic to an unsuspecting Cleaver, telling him we should attack the black nationalists who were against us in San Francisco and Oakland. I was Eldridge Cleaver's constant companion and he was now the leader of the Panthers. Cleaver wanted to use guns and put the other black nationalists out of commission. I was against that and lied to O'Connor and Kizenski. I told them that Cleaver had decided to start beating up the other black nationalists, including pistol whipping them.

Cleaver put out the word to the Panthers (there were still, actually, only about thirty hardcore members; the Free Huey Campaign would be the ticket to flood the membership roll) to start beating and pistol whipping other black nationalists. Contrary to what the FBI agents had hoped for, there was no retaliation from the other black groups. This campaign of terror continued for the next few months, running many of the black extremists who supported revolution out of the San Francisco Bay area.

However, with the white Communists and radicals supporting the Black Panther Party, the Huey Newton "cause celebre" began to draw thousands of supporters, and the black youth began to swell the ranks of the BPP in San Francisco and Oakland. It became a national media event.

Kizenski and O'Connor had no answer for the phenomenon and decided the only way to counteract it was to start internal strife inside the BPP itself. They told me to ask Cleaver to transfer me to Los Angeles to start a chapter down there, where I could be an independent leader inside the Panthers.

I asked Eldridge Cleaver to transfer me to Los Angeles, where I could start a Black Panther Party chapter. Cleaver's decision didn't come instantly, but finally in January, 1968, he sent me to Los Angeles. There we met a buddy of his from the penitentiary, Bunchy Carter, who Cleaver wanted to assist me in starting the Los Angeles chapter of the Black Panther Party.

CHAPTER IV

Divide and Destroy

I came back to Los Angeles in January, 1968. In my talks with Cleaver before leaving the Bay Area, I had encouraged him to wage an ideological war with Ron Karenga's US organization. This is what my FBI men, O'Connor and Kizenski, wanted. Cleaver agreed with my program.

The first meeting I went to was at the Black Congress on Broadway in South Central Los Angeles. Bunchy was with me, with our visibly armed bodyguard, Terry.

We stood out front and watched Karenga's army, running laps and practicing karate outside. Then Bunchy, Terry, and I went inside.

Karenga came in later. A large bald headed dressed man in a dashiki, he had two bodyguards with him dressed in similar clothing. All the Black Congress members in the room, about twenty, stood when he came in. We remained standing as well, and that is when I realized he was definately the new leader of black nationalists, at least in Los Angeles.

During the meeting, Bunchy and Terry went to the bathroom where they ran into members of the US organization—and Bunchy and Terry castigated them on their way of dressing saying: "You bald headed niggas with African earrings in your ear are gonna be run out of LA by the Panthers."

I had known Karenga from when he was Ron Everett, and we both were students at Los Angeles City College. I did not want warfare with my old friend, but the FBI did, and when I reported to them about Bunchy and Terry's confrontation with Karenga's people, they told me to take it a few steps farther, and incite Bunchy who was an ex-gang leader, to recruit his friends who were former gang members into the Panthers and start a war in the streets with Karenga's US group.

I exaggerated the US confrontation with Cleaver, telling him the word in the streets among black militants was that Karenga was not going to let the Panthers invade his turf. Cleaver was furious and told me to "roll over Karenga in Los Angeles." The word had been given by the new leader of the Black Panther Party and I gave his message to Bunchy, and told him to organize former members of his Slausons street gang into the Black Panthers and we were going to move on Karenga.

Within a few weeks, Bunchy organized close to a hundred young blacks and gave the orders to start jumping members of US. By this time they had considerable fewer members than we did. The FBI had asked me to have Panthers use guns, but I lied to them saying we might lose too many men we needed to fight the police. They reluctantly went for my lie because of Cleaver.

Walt Bremond, a fortyish black man who I knew from the San Francisco area and who was Chairman of the LA Black Congress wanted peace. He approached Karenga and Bunchy and me about having peace talks to stop the fighting.

O'Connor and Kizenski kept pushing me to convince Cleaver to resort to guns, and were upset when I broke the news to them that Cleaver had come under the influence of some white radical thinking from the Peace and Freedom Party, which was considering running him for President in 1968, and that he wanted me and Bunchy to sit down and work out a peace agreement with Karenga.

They had to momentarily go along with me, at least until

they could think of another plan.

Bunchy and I met with Karenga at his African artifact laden headquarters in South Central Los Angeles. In a tense meeting, we agreed to a truce, and to try to put a stop to the violence.

When I met again with my "shadows" a few days later at the Santa Monica pier, they had a new plan. To restart the violence they would send dummy letters to Karenga saying that the Panthers were going to kill him; and to myself and Bunchy who were then Deputys of Defense and Information respectively of the Panthers saying the same thing.

I'm not sure those letters were ever sent. However, as we shall see, similar letters were sent later. Cleaver instituted the riots again.

Aside from teaching political education classes, I was now giving fund-raising speeches to mostly middle classed liberal or radical white Peace and Freedom Party groups in Los Angeles; and I had a weekly fifteen minute politcal opinion show on KPFK-FM radio; and to the displeasure of the FBI, had been named a consultant to the director of the federally funded Economic Opportunity Program in Los Angeles, and had enrolled at West Los Angeles Law School, to finished my final year. O'Connor and Kizenski felt this sort of activity took up too much of my time, time that they felt I should be devoted following their orders and stirring up trouble among the "black extremists."

Eventually, O'Connor and Kizenski went along with my personal ambitions because they had bugged my apartment, and my phone, along with the few other high officials in the Black Panthers. And they also knew that Cleaver, who unofficially ran the Panthers, was highly in favor of what he considered to be my "establishment" pursuits which he felt would gain the Panthers favorable publicity.

A delegation of Panthers went to New York to the UN to demonstrate for the release of Huey P. Newton because they felt he was a political prisoner. I was in that delegation.

It was the summer of 1968 and the "shadows" knew that

Cleaver and Bobby Seale wanted the Student Nonviolent Coordinating Committee (SNCC) to become part of us. They knew that Stokely Carmichael was a friend of Cleaver's and was going to join the Black Panther Party. They also knew through the tapping of conversations with James Forman, H. Rap Brown, and myself that they were about to back out of an earlier agreement that would have made them officials of the Panthers and bring SNCC under Black Panther rule.

H. Rap Brown and Forman were going public with the statements that SNCC was backing out because Forman wisely feared retaliation from the Panthers. O'Connor and Kizenski knew this, and told me that they wanted me to convince Cleaver and Seale that Forman and Brown were going to the Black Muslims to get protection and were backing down from the deal to merge with the Black Panther Party.

I told Cleaver and Seale on the plane to New York that Forman, who was founder of SNCC, had said that he was going to seek the help of black Muslims to protect them so SNCC could stop the deal.

When our delegation got to New York, we were met by New York Panthers, numbering about two hundred, and their leader Will Pennywell.

Cleaver, Seale, David Hillard, and myself met with Stokely Carmichael our first night there. Cleaver and Seale were furious when Carmichael confirmed that Forman and H. Rap Brown were getting the Muslims to protect them and wanted no more to do with the Panthers.

Later, after some discussion, it was suggested that we kill Carmichael, Brown and Forman. I kept quiet during this discussion and my lack of enthusiasm brought a cold stare from Cleaver. I then expressed concern about the suggested killings—and the retaliation it might bring.

Cleaver made his decision. He, Seale, myself, Hillard and two or three other Panthers would visit Forman's house that night. We would leave Carmichael and Brown out of it because their fame as black leaders and to harm them might ignite an all out war. I felt that we were in danger of doing that in any case; and of course that would be exactly what O'Connor and Kizenski had been hoping for—and trying to get me to instigate all along.

That night we visited Forman as planned; and all of us were armed with pistols, knowing Forman did not carry a gun. I know the FBI had Forman bugged and would hear every word that went down. Later, they gloatingly told me that their seeds of dissention were spreading everywhere.

Cleaver, in his regular cool manner, came to the point with Forman, by accusing him of trying to start a was between the Panthers and the Muslims. Forman, a fortyish man, in mock disbelief, laughed. This infuriated Cleaver, who then ordered him to play Russian Roulette with two of our bodyguards.

The two Panthers put pistols to Forman's head, and began to pull the trigger on empty barrels, although Forman didn't know this. He screamed for his life, as Cleaver taunted him with insults.

Within a couple of days we had left New York, but it was clear to me that the FBI's plan of dissension, which they were using me to implement, was going to cause bloodshed within the movement.

It gets hot in August in Los Angeles, and it was so in '68. A presidential campaign loomed, Vietnam was escalating, and there was the prospect of another series of riots. I was continuing my teaching of political education at Black Panther headquarters when I heard the news. It came by radio that three Panthers had been shot and killed by police on Adams Boulevard—and one of the policemen was wounded while another Panther member had escaped.

I quickly drove to the scene of the killings, but it was crawling with spectators and police. I called Bunchy, and he told me that it was Steve, Robert and Little Tommy, all Captians of the BPP, who had been killed. Little Tony was with them and had shot the the two cops, but had come by Bunchy's apartment and had given him the details of the bloody affair.

I asked Bunchy where Little Tony was and he told me that he had given him the name of one of our white radical friends—he was escaping to Cuba that night.

I broke the rule and called the FBI. O'Connor and Kizenski were not in so I called Bunchy back. He told me that the Panther headquarters were surrounded by police and he wanted to set up our command post at my place. I agreed for him to use my apartment.

Within the hour, Bunchy, his bodyguard, Sherwin Fortier, and Captain Shermont Banks came to my apartment. We had several machine guns in the apartment and Bunchy came in talking some John Wayne movie type shit about making a last stand.

It looked like he was going to be right, however, for over thirty police cars lined the block where we were, and Bunchy, Sherwin, and Banks hotly proclaimed that we were going to have a show down with them, and that I had to go along with the program.

Then a call came from a black radio station, which wanted a statement from our spokesman—me—so I gave a heated comment to the effect of that the police had surrounded my apartment and was trying to kill the leadership of the Panthers in LA and that the LA Black Panthers were calling for protracted war on the police.

Within the hour several radio stations and newspapers called and I gave them statements that were much the same as my first one. The police were still waiting outside.

A couple of hours later the radio stations began broadcasting my statements. The police pulled out.

We stayed the night in my apartment and the next day Bobby Seale came down from Oakland. Bobby, Bunchy, and I gave interviews to the news media. That night Bobby and I gave an emotional speech to a crowd of thousands of blacks at a street corner rally at the scene of the killing of the three Black Panthers. When I met with the O'Connor and Kizenski at our designated time, they strangely were not upset with me, but were glad that I was assuming a leadership role. They said they were tired of the "Panther shit," and the FBI had worked out a deal with Karenga where they would supply US with weapons and a master plan to destroy the LA Black Panther Party; and they were looking to get something like that going in New York.

Within the week I got a call from Cleaver to come back to the Bay Area because the Panther Central Committee wanted me to accompany Kathleen Cleaver to Hawaii and Japan on a speaking tour.

I was substituting for Eldridge, who was supposed to have gone to Hawaii with Kathleen for the founding convention of the Peace and Freedom Party there. He was to be nominated as the presidential candidate for that state. Then he and Kathleen had been invited to make a speaking tour of Japan, sponsored by *Beherein*, an organization of Japanese writers and artists. This tour was to conincide with a month of conferences in protest of the war in Vietnam and nuclear weapons. At the last minute, however, the parole board had slapped a travel ban on him.

I went to San Francisco August 9, 1968. Elridge met me at the airport and both of us went to the dining room there where we had a short meeting with Paul Jacobs, writer and participant in radical causes, who was also a Peace and Freedom Party California senatorial candidate. After that, we left the airport and went back to Eldridge's house on Pine Street.

For the next hour or so, Eldridge and I talked about the situation in Los Angeles as it then stood, and the questions that might be raised on this international tour. It was to be the Party's first venture into this arena, so what had to be accomplished politically was to make the people of Japan see the parallels between our struggles and the way it was being waged in the United States, and the Third World struggles. This was made difficult by the tricky questions of land—that is, are blacks fighting for land or separate states; the transitional nature of black organizations; our earlier preoccupation with non-violence as the major ideological tenet, and so on and so forth. There was no pat answers to these questions, but Elridge felt the concerned people of Japan could be made to see that we were breaking new theoretical ground in the struggle of oppressed people around the world. The problems of the Third World are basically the same, only our strategy and tactics had to be different to fit the situation.

Kathleen and I caught a United Airlines flight at about three that afternoon. The trip to Hawaii took about five hours.

There was a good sized delegation at the airport to meet us, and they carried signs saying "Welcome to Hawaii," and threw leis around our necks. There were also several cops standing around in the background, back away from the official delegation. Newspaper photographers kept asking us to pose for pictures and we gave a television interview on the spot.

We left the airport and were taken to the home of the Joe Murphy's, a very spacious, attractive house on top of one of the many hills of the island. There was a cocktail party in our honor, which was already in progress by the time we got there.

After the reception, Kathleen and I were taken to the home of John and Mary Kelly, which was on the beach.

That night Kathleen Cleaver spoke at McKinley Auditorium. There were over a thousand people there.

The next day, Saturday, Kathleen and I were scheduled to leave for the orient. Kathleen spoke at the Peace and Freedom Party convention that afternoon, giving an acceptance speech for Eldridge. Then we rushed to the Japanese consulate to get our visas. They told us on the phone that it would only be a matter of filling out a few forms, and would take less than an hour to complete.

When we got to the office around three o'clock, we were the only ones there. The consul came from behind his desk, gave us forms to fill our, and went back to his desk to read his afternoon newspaper. I was filling out a form when out of the corner of my eye I saw hm look up from the paper at us, then back to the paper again, and then with an expression of disbelief look up at us again.

I knew what he had seen. The Honolulu *Advertiser* had run a front page six column story about our trip, with individual pictures of us. I watched him quickly read the story, his face mirroring his intense shock.

When we finished our forms and had turned them over to him, he checked our names and I knew his worst fears had been proven true. His hands trembled as he read the names on the forms to himself.

Then he started the evasion act. It might take a little time, he said. He would have to wire his home office in Tokyo for an okay on our visas, since we could not be classified as tourists, or on business of a "regular sort."

Since it was obvious that he was going to put us uptight, we decided we might as well be as difficult as possible. He was a quiet type of man, and it was easily seen that our complaints and accusations of imperialist-inspired deceit and unfairness caused him great discomfort and a certain amount of personal embarrassment.

He was sweating when he got back to his desk, but it did not hamper him from carrying through his mission. Tapping out a wire to Tokyo, he then told us he would have an answer by that night and would contact us. But I knew that he was just trying to get us to leave the premises peacefully, and that it was going to be a problem trying to get permission to visit Japan.

That night he called to say that he was having trouble getting clearance on our visas. The next day the Honolulu *Bulletin* carried a story outlining our trouble. We relaxed and prepared to stay a few more days to see how things worked out, and then probably go home.

On that day, we placed a call to the Beherein organization in Japan, telling them what happened. Beherein promised to immediately organize a demonstration in front of the Japanese Foreign Ministry and the American Embassy, protesting the Japanese governments's refusal to issue the visas. They had thousands of people participating in the conference, which was by now in full swing. The demonstration took place Monday morning in Tokyo—Sunday in Hawaii. Our visas were immediately okayed. Meanwhile, Kathleen had decided to return to San Francisco. I never did know the reason she suddenly decided to go home. Perhaps there was no reason, or maybe Eldridge, for whatever reason he had, told her to come back to San Francisco and not go on to Japan with me. I was to make the trip alone.

Opposite: Huey Newton in court for the last time, on March 14, 1989. Overleaf 1: The "Free Huey" rally at Alameda County courthouse on July 17, 1968. Overleaf 2: The April 26, 1968 shootout between the Black Panthers and the Oakland police. Overleaf 3: The Black Panthers were accused of staging a holdup from the pictured van in which three Oakland police officers were wounded on November 19, 1968. Overleaf 4: Huey Newton on August 4, 1970 after finally being released from jail. Overleaf 5: Eldridge Cleaver at a "Free Huey" rally at the University of California at Berkeley on October 8, 1968. All photographs reprinted by permission of the Oakland Tribune.

CHAPTER V

Caught Between The Panthers and The FBI

It was Monday night when I arrived in Tokyo. At the airport I picked up an English edition of a Japanese newspaper. They'd printed a large picture on the front page of the demonstration in front of the Foreign Ministry. I learned later that none of the other American delegations there, SNCC and SDS (Students for a Democratic Society) included, had encountered the problems that we had in getting visas.

I was staying at the Hotel Dai Ichi, and the next day John Wilson, former Deputy Chairman of SNCC, whom I had known before also checked in. That afternoon, the Japanese radicals corralled us, along with Ken Cloak of SDS, while we were attempting a sightseeing tour of the countryside, and occupied our entire day with political discussions. Since John Wilson, Ken Cloak and I were coming from the same place, more or less, but looked at the problems we were trying to get solved in a different light, it was not easy to make the Japanese radicals (mostly students) understand. They kept insisting that we should be able to forget our differences, join forces and work from the same place.

The radical left student movement in Japan at that time was very large, and itself very diversified. The largest and what was considered the "main" group was called the Zengakuren, which was further split into numerous factions.

There were pro-Maoists, anti-Maoists, Trotskyites, Stalinists, and numerous other groups. During my political tour there, each of the factions in turn approached me to ask me to speak in one of their forums. The sponsoring faction would always ask me leading questions, which were geared to bring a response from me that would be an ideological attack upon the other factions. Sometimes they didn't bother attempting to be sophisticated about it; at one interview the Trotskyites attacked the Stalinists and asked me, at least in principle, to agree with their attack.

When John and I were interviewed one night, I was asked one loaded question that was to come up time and again while I was in Japan—the reports that there is a feud between the Panthers and SNCC.

There had been an incident the previous month when the Panthers, myself included, had gone to New York on a mission that was supposed to take us to the United Nations to present the facts about Huey Newton's case; and to demand plebiscite. The UN visit turned out to be a failure, and so did the attempt to intimidate SNCC by threatening leader James Forman's life. I lied to the groups that asked me about this, saying I knew nothing of a threat.

I spoke to many groups. Actually, the main action of the conference was taking place away from Tokyo in the villages of the countryside, where each city would host a conference of two or three days. A body of thousands, Japanese and foreigners alike, were moving from city to city. My hosts, however, were still preparing my intinerary, since certain adjustments had to be made because of my late arrival.

I was scheduled to speak in Osaka on the fourth day. I was the final speaker on the program, more or less the keynote speaker, following a series of introductions and short speeches designed to excite the crowd. I decided that my emphasis would be on the question of racism being a major problem in Third World nations. I opened as I always did by stating that our leader, Huey P. Newton, was a political prisoner and above all else, my party was demanding that he be set free.

Then I continued by outlining the problems of black America and of people of color around the world were facing, consisting mostly of racism and economic exploitation.

The following day I spoke to a smaller group at the conference and left that evening for Okinawa, which then was a US protectorate, as well as being the major American nuclear air base in the Far East. I spoke at several small caucuses and gave several newspaper and magazine interviews.

Three days later I returned to Tokyo for media interviews and then returned to the States. (This Japan tour was covered in my incomplete CIA files; incomplete because they did not include the dealings with secret operations of the Agency.)

I then came back to LA, and waiting for me was a registered letter from O'Connor and Kizenski, which ordered to contact them by phone, and gave me several different times that I would be able to reach them.

I made contact and we met the following day. They informed me that they knew, through bugging the headquarters, that the Black Panther Party wanted me to speak at the Democratic Convention in Chicago coming up within a week or so—August 26 through September 9. They suggested instead that I get out of the country for a few weeks because Mayor Richard Daly's police forces planned to come down hard on white radicals and Panthers, who had plans to disrupt the Convention and also planned to demonstrate against the war in Vietnam.

I did some fast thinking and told O'Connor and Kizenski that I was going to Rome to visit my friend, Vonetta McGee. Of course, I hadn't been invited but knew Vonetta was there making a film—and that they probably knew that. I had met Vonetta at the Black House when she had been a student at San Francisco State, where she was a theater major and also a political activist. It was Vonetta who'd picked me up from San Francisco Internationl when I'd returned there after Huey was shot.

Vonetta was in Italy making her film debut in a spaghetti

western—in which she was playing a Mexican woman, as it turned out. She would go on to star in such films as *The Big Silence, The Eiger Sanction, Shaft in Africa, Blacula, The Lost Man* (with Sidney Poitier), *The Kremlin Letter* and dozens of others, including *Brothers* in which she played a character based on Angela Davis. Eventually she turned her attention to stage where she has done many roles, including starring in the Woody King, Jr. production of Ron Milner's *Seasons Reasons.*

An extraordinarily beautiful woman, Vonetta was born in Mississippi but her political awareness was sharpened in San Francisco at the time of the Black House and the Panthers.

As it turned out, Vonetta had an apartment in Rome but she was away in the countryside on location. I was in Rome several days, staying at Vonetta's place, and I did nothing politically. When I came back from Rome I checked in with O'Connor and Kizenski, and they told me that the FBI planned to bring the notch of struggle against the Black Panther Party up a level. Huey Newton—after a a seven week long trial that ended on September 9—had only been convicted of manslaughter, rather than murder as the Establishment had hoped and expected. Since Huey had had his day in court and was now to serve his time, the FBI felt that the Free Huey movement was history. Now they intended to concentrate on putting an end to the white radical "End the War in Vietnam" movement. They also told me that Elridge Cleaver was going to jail for the shootout with the Oakland police back on the night of April 6-7 when Little Bobby had been killed. This was during the trouble that followed the murder of Dr. Martin Luther King, Jr. in Memphis.

In an encounter with two Oakland policemen, Eldridge and Little Bobby Hutton had been forced into a house on 28th Street in Oakland (we later referred to it as the Battle of 28th Street), after the policemen, who were in a patrol car, opened fire on them. Calling for reinforcements, soon some fifty Oakland police were on the scene with minutes. Tear gas was fired into the house, forcing Little Bobby and Eldridge to take their chances on the outside. They called out that they were going to surrender, and threw out a rifle. They came out, and Little Bobby was helping Eldridge who had been hit in the leg with a tear gas cannister.

One of the cops pushed Little Bobby away from Eldridge, and told him to run toward a squad car which had a door open. Little Bobby ran, according to what Eldridge, and others who were there, told us later, with his arms in the air. The police opened fire and blew him to eternity.

A crowd of black people had gathered and saw Little Bobby cruelly baited into running. They vigorously condemned the police with shout of "Murderers, murderers!"

No doubt that outcry against the cold-blooded shooting of Little Bobby Hutton was what saved Eldridge's life; that and the fact the Eldridge was as naked as the day he'd come into this world. He'd expected an ambush when he came out of the house and removed all his clothing before coming out of the house. He'd tried to get Little Bobby to do the same thing, but being only seventeen and modest, he'd refused. It cost him his life because the police would later claim they'd thought he had a concealed weapon.

I really loved Little Bobby and I think everyone in the Party did. Little Bobby's funeral was held April 13, 1968 at Ephesiams Church of God in Christ in Berkeley. Three-hundred Panthers attended the service, dressed in the BPP uniform. National, and local political officials attended as did celebrities, including Marlon Brando who had shown sympathy for the Panther cause.

Eldridge had been arrested and stayed in jail for fifty days before getting out on bail. He'd been out only a short time when we went to New York to demonstrate for the "Free Huey" movement and to confront SNCC, as related above.

O'Connor and Kizenski said, with both Eldridge and Huey out of the way serving time, they were going to crush the Panthers. They said they were going to pay FBI street informants, and make a deal to exonerate their lesser crimes, if they would join the Black Panther Party. The objective was to start an internecine struggle to destroy the Party. They were also interested in finding out who would lead the Black Panther Party, once Eldridge Cleaver was put in jail, and out of the way. The BPP now had over 3,000—most of them, of course, having joined since Huey had been jailed—members across the country, and was considered a formidable political and military force.

They wanted me to go to New York and try to get a contract to write a book about my Panther experiences and to use that as a vehicle to gain leadership of the Party. I was able to get a recommendation from author James Baldwin, which opened doors for me in New York. I easily acquired an agent, and got a deal with the Dial Press—for a lot more money than I'd even hoped for—to write a book on my experiences in the Black Panther Party. It was early in October, 1968 when I left to go back to Oakland to tell the Central Committee of the Black Panther Party about the book. I had the idea they would welcome the chance for someone on the inside to tell the story from our point of view.

First, however, I traveled back to Los Angeles and told the news of the book contract to O'Connor and Kizenski. They were pleased, of course. From there I flew to San Francisco to break what I thought of as the "good news" to the Panthers. I thought I would get the approval of the leadership with little or no trouble, and the Feds thought also thought there would be no problem.

I was wrong. Cleaver was totally against the idea of my doing a book on the Panthers under any circumstances. I suspected, at the time, he wanted to be the only published writer within the BPP leadership. At any rate, his highhanded attitude caught me completely off guard.

To make matters worse, I was put under house arrest by the Party for being an opportunist. I was to stay at the home of David Hillard, under the control of the three members of the elite military army, the Black Guard. Needless to say, this turn of events was totally unexpected. There seemed to be a second problem; the contents of my speeches in Japan, which dealt heavily with racism, had been severely criticized and particulary by Eldridge Cleaver. I accepted his right to criticize, as well as that of other high officials of the Party, for the criticism was based on sound political logic. It was somewhere around that time the Party was formulating its political ideology based on an analysis of society in terms of class exploitation, but I did and could not accept this ideology.

On the second day of my house arrest, I asked the Guard members who were holding me imprisoned to pick up some marijuana to smoke. They agreed. I had called ahead to my renegade Muslim brothers: Alonzo, James X, Abdul, and Sam X to tell them to get ready to rescue me if I could get these three to bring me over to Alonzo's apartment. I'd first met these Muslim brothers when I moved to San Francisco from Los Angeles and became a Muslin convert myself. We lived together and, as a group, could not really follow the strict laws against drinking, smoking dope and womanizing the Muslims required of its members, and that is why we were "renegade Muslims."

We did go over to the apartment they still shared. When we arrived, I went to the door with my three guards and knocked.

Alonzo X came to the door and asked who was there. I told him. He asked us to wait, and several minutes later, he opened the door with a sawed-off shotgun, and with James, Abdul, and Sam X, backing him up, all armed with shotguns. They were in Fruit of Islam dress regalia, and told the Panthers that they were taking me in the name of Islam. I was rescued and will always be grateful to my fellow renegade Muslim brothers for saving my life.

The next day I left the Bay Area to go to Los Angeles to meet with Kizenski and O'Connor and tell them what had transpired, and find out what I should do next. I had a feeling that my escaping was not going to go down too well with the Black Panther higher command. We met at the Santa Monica pier, and they told me I was going to New York. They had telephone taps on headquarters in San Francisco, Los

Angeles, New York, and Chicago—and from the information they'd overhead, they felt that going to New York and being around H. Rap Brown was the best chance I had of surviving. Brown, the firey leader of SNCC, liked me.

I went to New York, and was followed there a few weeks later by O'Connor and Kizenski. I stayed at the apartment of a friend, Gene Lewis, and began to hang out at the Manhattan office of SNCC with H. Rap Brown and James Forman. At night I spent a lot of time at Pee Wee's bar and with Shelley, who was a barmaid there.

Stokely Carmichael came through New York with his wife, African singer Miriam Makeba; who was doing an engagement at the Appollo. Stokely contacted me and told me of a plan he wanted me to get involved in.

He wanted me to assist him in pulling a *coup d'etat* on the Panthers in Oakland. He wanted for us to convince the New York chapter to follow us to Africa, to Guinea, where he lived with his wife. From there, we would train a land army of Panthers to go down to the country of Ghana to take charge of the government by force. Prime Minister Osaygefo Kwame Nkrumah, who in exile in Guinea, had been Carmichael's tutor.

I ran Carmichael's plan past the FBI at a meeting in Central Park. They thought Stokely's plan would cause a disruption that seemed to dovetail with some greater plan that someone was working on and told me to agree to do whatever Carmichael asked. They said they would have the word spread to the informants instructing them to follow Carmichael and myself.

Carmichael and I met several times that week with the leadership of the New York Black Panther chapter in a small, dingy apartment. He outlined the plan, and told the leadership, which later became the notorious New York 21, (and after that the even more notorious Black Liberation Army), that he was leaving for Africa, but I would be his man in the States. I was to be in charge of building the army in New York, along with his brother, Field Marchall Donald Cox.

Carmichael and I then went to Honolulu, Hawaii, where both of us spoke to capacity crowds. Then we returned to New York, where we were joined with his wife, Miriam and went to Montreal for a black writers' conference. I had the blessings of my FBI men to make these trips with Carmichael.

When I returned from Canada, I talked to the O'Connor and Kizenski. They told me the Panthers were heavily infiltrated by informants in Los Angeles, New York, Oakland, and Chicago, and that I should go ahead with their original plan (and which was the same as the plan Stokely had come up with) of taking over the leadership of the Black Panthers by controlling the New York chapter.

I talked to Rap Brown about it, but he hadn't forgotten how Carmichael had treated James Forman badly in the past, and didn't want to get involved in any of his plans.

It was November of 1968 and word was put out by the Oakland Panthers and got back to my agent's office in New York, and WBAI radio station, where I was doing political commentary, that I had been silenced by the BPP. I had also been placed under suspension for leaving my post in Los Angeles as well as, they said, for the inability to submit to discipline.

I still continued to have clandestine meetings with different groups of Panthers who were loyal to me and agreed with the ideas of myself and Carmichael, who was now back in Africa.

It was the latter part of December that my FBI shadows gave me the word. The Black Panther Party in Oakland had a contract to kill out on me, and that I should get out of the country and write my book.

I talked to H. Rap Brown about the contract on my life, and leaving the country. We were sitting on a park bench in Central Park, and his response was that he could organize some Black Muslims to retaliate. I nixed the idea as being too dangerous. Rap said he would arrange for some contacts for me in Europe.

On January 18, 1969, I read in the New York *Times* that

Bunchy Carter and John Jerome Huggins had been shot to death in a cafeteria at UCLA. It was reporrted that the shooting was result of a feud with rival Los Angeles organization, Ron Karenga's US, and the Panthers.

Well, yes it was; the same fued that had been suggested and abetted, if not planned (I have no idea who came up with the idea) by O'Connor and Kizenski when I was still working with Bunchy in Los Angeles. Eleven years later, when I got copies of my FBI files, it contained a memorandum from "SAC, Los Angeles" to "Director, FBI" dated 11/29/68. It headed Operations under Consideration" and stated: "The Los Angeles Office is currently preparing an anonymous letter for Bureau approval which will be sent to the Los Angeles Black Panther Party (BPP) supposed from a member of the 'US' organization in which it will be stated that the youth group of the 'US' organization is aware of the BP 'contract' to kill RON KARENGA, leader of 'US', and they, 'US' members, in retaliation, have made plans to ambush leaders of the BPP in Los Angeles.

"It is hoped this counterintellingence (sic) measure will result in an "US" and BPP vendetta.

"Investigation has indicated that the Peace and Freedom Party (PFP) has been furnishing the BPP with financial assistance. An anonymous letter is being prepared for Bureau approval to be sent to a leader of PFP in which it is set forth that the BPP has made statements in closed meetings that when the armed rebellion comes the whites in the PFP will be lined up against the wall with the rest of the whites.

"It is felt that this type of a letter could cause considerable disruption of the association between the BPP and the PFP.

"In order to cause disruption between the BPP of Oakland, California, and the BPP of Los Angeles, an envelope is being prepared for Bureau approval which appears to have been prepared and distributed by the Los Angeles BPP soliciting donations for defense of HUEY NEWTON and to be mailed to the mailing address of Carl Earl Leon Anthony, Deputy Minister of Information, or Los Angeles headquarters. This envelope, with a small donation, will be inadvertently sent to the BPP in Oakland.

"It is hoped that the BPP in Oakland would get the impression that a considerable amount of money was being collected in Los Angeles and not sent to the Oakland headquarters..."

The memo then contains six paragraphs under the heading of "Operations Being Effected" that deal with swaying opinion aganist the BPP in the "Negro community"; the mailing of a "prepared letter" to Joudon Ford of the New York Panthers "in the hopes of furthering discord between CLEAVER and the New York BPP" outlining other ways to persecute BPP leaders. The three-page memo closed with the following paragraph: "Friction between the BPP and 'US' continues in the Los Angeles area with RON KARENGA and JAMES LEROY DOSS, another 'US' leader, slated to be killed. BPP leders feel that their new member, DON WATTS, has been instructed by 'US' to infiltrate the BPP and report back to 'US'. The BPP continues in their efforts to take over the leadership of the black nationalist movement. The Los Angeles Office will utilzie every technique to capitalize on this development and hinder the BPP's efforts in this regard."

This memo was dated November 29, 1968. Six weeks later, on January 18, 1969, Alprentice "Bunchy" Carter and Jerome Higgins (who had replaced me as Deputy Minister of Information), were shot to death at the UCLA cafeteria. It was reported that they never had a chance and the shooting was the result of a feud with Ron Karenga's US. There is no doubt in my mind but what the murders were carried out by US members, nor that it was a direct result of the "feud" abetted by the FBI.

I went to Paris the first week in March, 1969 with plans of writing my book. I stayed in Paris with two young political activists, who have been active both in Europe and Africa, M. and Mme. Herve. Julia Herve is the former Julia Wright, daughter of the late great black author Richard Wright.

Julia arranged for me to speak twice while I was in Paris,

and to give a major press conference.

While there, I kept up with the activities of the Panthers by reading the Party newspaper. It was March 1969 when I first learned of the purge of Party membership of people considered to be counterrevolutionary, opportunists, adventurists, etc. Each week in the Panther paper, names of people purged were listed. I recognized many of the names as top officials, deeply involved in Panther activities; and when I called O'Connor and Kizenski, stateside, they told me that the purge was about serious killings of people inside the Party thought to be informants.

In the early part of April, 1969, I went to Uppsala, Sweden, a small university city outside of Stockholm. I completed my book, but in the book I did not go into the fact that I was myself an informant.

It was later, June of 1969, when one of the blacks there showed me a copy of the March 29, 1969 Party paper in which the Panthers made countless vicious accusations against me, and closed the article by issuing their version of an "all points bulletin" requesting information about my whereabouts.

I left Sweden, where I had been living with a lover, Siv, in early July, going to London.

I was to stay there until November. I stayed with a young Anglo woman named June and worked as a public relations director for an African dramatic company.

I came back to the States in December 1969 and met with Kizenski and O'Connor who told me the Panthers, the black movement, and the anti-Vietnam movement were disintegrating.

After a couple of weeks of Manhatten, I went to Roanoke, where I stayed until March when my book was published.

CHAPTER VI

Becoming Famous Is Dangerous To One's Health

It was about six forty-five in the morning and I was in the wings, waitng to go onstage to be interviewed by NBC's *Today Show*. It was March in Manhattan and the year was 1970. I felt strangely good an about the world and myself. I'd had some vistors the night before—by the name of O'Connor and Kizenski—but even they had not been able to dampen my spirits. Anyway, it seemed to me they were talking and I wasn't hearing. They went on and on, about the BPP, the Mafia, this sting and that operation. I was supposed to be paying attention to this? I was going on national television the next morning, to be interviewed by one of the most famous women in America. Actually, even my FBI shadows seemed excited about that. Some how they'd figured that I'd be more valuable to them by becoming famous.

I had turned thirty that month and my first book, and my memoirs about my experiences as a member of the Black Panther Party had just been published. At that time the BBP membership had reached five thousand and the Party was being called "Public Enemy Number One" by FBI Director J. Edgar Hoover.

The book was called *Picking Up the Gun*, and it was an honest effort—up to a point. It was honest enough that the then leadership of the BBP, an inner circle of which I had once been a member, had put a price on my life. However, in retrospect, *Picking Up The Gun* doesn't seem all that honest to me; I told enough of the truth to have a very commerical book on my hands; I deliberately omitted some very important details because I was not only protecting myself and my family—who had also been threatened—but out of some sense of loyalty I was also protecting those people I joined up with as an original Black Panther.

When I was introduced to Barbara Walters, she said, "You don't look like a Black Panther."

I was dressed in a blue pinstripe double breasted suit with powder blue shirt, maroon tie, and Pierre Cardin shoes. At the time I was wearing a trim beard and goatee. And talking to me was the top-rated female anchor woman in the country, looking much lovelier that you see her on television.

I replied, "I am, though."

When my interview—fifteen minutes—came up, Barbara Walters suddenly and unexpectedly (at least to me) ferociously attacked me with her incisive style, wanting me to tell her about such things as Panthers killing other black nationalists; did the Panthers have a contract out to kill me because they felt I was an FBI informant; what about their threats against my publisher, my agents, and my employers, radio stations KPFK in Los Angeles and WBAI in New York, where I was a political commentator? Much of this had been reported in a feature in the New York *Times* earlier that week. I tried to be evasive in my answers but she wasn't buying that. I kept thinking, "this woman is trying to get me killed." She continued to hit me with her persistence; until co-host Edwin Newman called her off.

While I was leaving the studio, I asked her for her telephone number. I wanted a date with her. That's where my head was at the time. She gave me a number. When I called that night, and got no answer, I thought, "How do I deserve Barbara Walters? She must have given me a phony number."

(In my 666 pages of FBI files there is a transcript of the interview and although Edwin Newman is referred to by name, Ms. Walters is simply called the woman—either an example of FBI male chauvinism, or an editorial comment on how the Agency feels about Ms. Walters. I received my files in 1981 under the Freedom of Information Act. They date from 1967 to 1974.)

Picking Up the Gun: A Report on the Black Panthers was to become the best selling book at Dial Press, then a major New York house, in 1970, and it was published in paperback by Pyramid, and in France by Presence Africaine. It was reviewed in more than a hundred newspapers and magazines (I received a leather bound book from Dial for being the best selling author at the house for that year.)

At any rate, later that evening I went for a walk down the street to a bar I'd taken to hanging out in. It was pretty well known that the place was Mafia owned and pretty much of a hangout for the younger Mafioso. I hadn't gone two blocks when someone tried to kill me. I was walking facing the traffic, on the left sidewalk. A car came down the street toward me, slowly. Too slowly. It got my attention and I became suspicious. Since the Panthers had threatened my life I'd become a bit paranoid. Fortunatly I was on guard. A gloved hand slid out the window holding what looked like a .22. I yelled and hit the cement. I never did know why I yelled. At any rate, one shot was fired and came close enough that it threw cement dust into my eyes. The car sped off.

Across the street, what looked like a middle-aged white couple stopped for a moment, then walked on as if they saw black men get shot down in that quaint but nice section of Manhatten every night. Maybe they did. I got up and brushed myself off, thinking I should call the police. I'd really taken myself out of the revolution, I thought, when the first thing I could think of was call the police. And what would I say to the police? The Black Panther party is trying to kill me? Didn't you see me with Barbara Walters this morning? Or perhaps it is only the FBI that wants me dead? The Mafia, maybe? Those dudes at the bar where I sometimes hung out at in the East Village had been buying me a lot of drinks lately, and I'd had an offer to run drugs for them. I'm a celebrated writer and on a Black Panther hit list. On the other hand, perhaps the shooter thought I was someone else. Maybe he didn't care who I was; maybe he just wanted to shoot someone. Anyone. I'd known of that to happen. More than once.

Since no one had seemed to notice except for the couple who were now turning the next corner, walking as slowly as ever, and there had been no screams, no police sirens, I decided to go on down to the corner and think it over. Later, when I told people about it, no one seemed to believe me. It was hinted on more than one occasion that I was just trying to get publicity for my book.

It was the month before, May, and I was back in New York waiting for my book to come out, when the Mafia ran the "looper" at me. I had a friend who was a barmaid at Pee Wee's jazz nightclub and restaurant in Manhattan's Lower East Village. Her name was Shelley, and she was a diminutive black spitfire, very popular at the club—in fact with the entire New York night scene.

A "looper" is what it is called when the Mafia checks you out, to see if they want to pick you up to work for them, or decide that you are not "cut out" for the Mafioso style.

I'd met Shelley through Gene Lewis, a tall man with a shaven head who was working as the host/bouncer of the earthy, sawdust floored jazz club. I was staying around the corner from Pee Wee's in Gene's apartment, which he let me use rent free, while he stayed with his lady, Toni Cade-Bambara, who was to become a well known writer/professor/intellectual. Gene Lewis was later to become one of New York's most popular male models.

I'd met Gene Lewis, first by telephone, when I'd taken a mutual friend's suggestion and called him. That was when I was in New York to do my book deal in the autumn of 1968. As it happened, he invited me to stay at his apartment. After that I stayed with Gene whenever I was in New York, at least until after my book was published. Shelley had taken a liking to me, particularly because I was a close friend of fellow black militant Stokely Carmichael, who was a year younger than me, and the father of Shelley's son, Kwame.

Upon returning to New York from abroad in late 1969, I decided to settle there. After visiting Roanoke for a month I settled into an apartment on Manhattan's Columbus Avenue and West 79th Street. I began to visit Shelley again at Pee Wee's.

One night after work, Shelly and I went to her apartment to talk. Shelley told me that the Mafia was interested in me getting involved in interstate narcotics dealing, transporting drugs from New York to the San Francisco Bay area. She said that the reason the Mafia wanted me to do this work was because I had been friends with many of the people who now made up the notorious Black Liberation Army, a paramilitary underground group of about twenty young black men and one woman, the leader, Jo Anne Chesimard. The B.L.A. was to kill several policemen and rob several banks between 1970 and 1974. Chesimard was later arrested for first degree murder of a highway patrolman in 1973, but escaped to Cuba in 1981.

I had told Shelley that I'd been associated with the B.L.A. in 1968 before they had become so well known.

Shelley told me one night, after I'd returned from Europe and and while I was waiting for my book to come out, that if I was interested in the drug deal the Mafia would provide me with a young black woman to have sex with each night that I wanted. They would be barmaids from New York nightclubs, bars, and restaurants that were Mafia owned. I told Shelley I would have to think it over. I really don't know why the offer seemed so tempting at the time. For one thing I was very nervous about how my book would be accepted, and for another, I was broke. I decided to leave the city to mull over the proposition.

I flew down to Roanoke, Virginia, where I was born. I stayed with my great aunt and uncle, James and Doris Witcher in a large-frame house in the black community in Virginia's third largest city. Here I had spent many an enjoyable summer in my youth, and spent one memorable fall when I was thirteen; summer days of playing Tarzan and seeing cowboy movies; and as a teenager in the fall of 1953 playing junior high school football.

But now I was in Roanoke in the spring of 1970, waiting for my first book to come out, and hiding out from the Black Panthers. They had contracted to kill me—this they announced to my agent, publisher, and both radio stations I was working for at the time. They had instructed all members and followers to look for me. It was openly stated, and believed by the Party, white radicals, and their followers, that I was not only an FBI informant, but the top FBI agent provocateur in the Panther Party—and in the 1960s movement.

I was to be in Roanoke for two weeks. I kept in contact with my agent, a young black named Ron Hobbs, and spent my days talking black liberation politics with my buddies, and early mornings taking long, solitary walks around the city, in an attempt to sort out my thoughts about going to work for the Mafia. I had just gotten out of the black revolution in America and I finally decided that I did not want to join the criminal underworld—even though I realized that they had a powerful set of legitimate businesses in America that could have propelled me to fame and fortune. But more importantly, I knew the FBI would be mad at me for reneging on my cover for them.

While in Roanoke I did an interview with the Roanoke *Times*, the city's largest newpaper, about my political views; and one night before I left, I wrote all night finishing two one-act plays, an hour's worth of stage. One of the plays was about a police informant living with the Black Panther Party. It was called *The Misjudgement*, and the other was a dark comedy about a confrontation between a Black Muslim and a Panther as they watched the Apollo landing on the moon. It was called *Charlie Still Can't Win No Wars on the Ground*.

After Two weeks, I left Roanoke and went back to New York. I contacted Shelley the day before I left and I told her I was undecided about joining the Mafia. She said she would relay he message through her contact. Shelley also asked me to come by the East Village bar the next day. I did and when I got there, she had a surprise party waiting for me to celebrate the publication of my book.

The bar and restaurant was crowded with an invitation only group of blacks, mostly jazz musicians and single ladies. Many of the jazz musicians lived in the East Village of Manhattan at that time. The bar was a favorite hangout for the jazz crowd.

It was to be a lively night of camaraderie. The jukebox played and the drinks were on the house, or at least free. The party livened up when a light skinned, shapely, bald-headed black woman named Boomer, accompanied by a black man named James, who Shelley introduced as her play brother. Boomer started showing nude pictures of herself around the party.

After the pictures of her were shown around, she sat on top of the bar and pulled up her dress. She was wearing no panties, and had a bare vulva. She announced: "I've got the prettiest pussy in New York! Who wants to eat it?"

I shouted: "I do."

Everybody laughed.

Boomer, James and I left the bar shortly after that, taking a cab to my apartment. James went to the bathroom; Boomer told me that he'd gone to shoot up some smack. Boomer and I went to the bedroom. She asked me to tie her to the bed with the sheets and fuck her. I did. She would cry out: "Harder! Harder!" I came three times, then Boomer and James left.

The next day I went to my agent's office to talk about my book. After the business conversation with Ron Hobbs, I was invited into the office of a nineteen year old high yellow black chick named Shyleen who worked for Hobbs. She told me that Robin Bruce, a five foot ten inch, voluptuously built, high yellow stunner, who wore an Afro hairdo, and worked for Hobbs as a receptionist, had a crush on me. Well, she happened not to be there that day. I had met Robin, though, and arranged with Shyleen to get together with her that night at the apartment they shared with their respective boyfriends, who, as it turned out, were New York Mafioso dope dealers and were now in California transporting narcotics. Later I found out they were also Vietnam veterans.

I went to the apartment to meet Robin that night. She was there with Shyleen and a friend named Sylvia Rhone. They were wearing Black Panther Party tee shirts. I guess they were trying to impress me. We snorted some coke. We talked casually, and then I left with Robin. We walked to my apartment, which was a short distance away, laughing and talking.

When we got there, Robin had some pot so I smoked some with her. I asked her to have sex with me, but she refused. I used a tactic that had become a fetish with women I partiularly loved; the reason for which I will explain later. I slapped her hard two or three times. She relented then, and I made her give me oral sex first and then I went inside of her.

Afterwards, we lay in bed talking. The doorbell rang and I wrapped a towel around me and picked up the the nine millimeter handgun that I carried. It was Boomer and James. Boomer was carryng a small overnight case. Boomer said that she had come to stay with me. I told her no deal. She and James left.

That night with Robin started a whirlwind relationship which was to lead to a short marriage.

The next morning I was awakened by a pounding on the door. Robin had left earlier, and only a few people knew where I lived. I went to the door clad only in my briefs—holding my gun in hand.

'Who goes?" I asked.

"Kizenski and O'Connor," answered the voice of my FBI contacts. Robert O'Connor, the well-built young blond, along with the equally handsome sandy haired Kizenski had been my contacts since 1967 when they recruited me in San Francisco.

Both men were part of the FBI counter intelligence squad

called COINTELPRO, which specialized in infiltraiting black extremists, revolutionaries and white radicals.

O'Connor and Kizenski worked out of Washington, D.C. but were more or less assigned to Los Angeles and San Francisco to keep an eye on radical black groups and, in particular, the Black Panther Party. They both had been in the Marines in Vietnam. They once told me that I was the first FBI informant in the COINTELPRO operation.

I had really been forced into the operation and now I wanted out, but they would not let me go. About once every month or so, they would visit me with a new assignment. Then I was to tell them of my progress via registered mail once a week.

The last time I had seen them was the night before I was interviewed on the *Today Show*—March of 1970. And now it was the first week of June.

I knew my phone and apartment were bugged, and probably the phones and apartments of all the women I had made love to, as well. So, I figured these two knew the Mafia had directly approached me with an offer about running drugs cross country.

In my letters to O'Connor and Kizenski, I had not mentioned the Mafia; I only talked about how I was trying to get national exposure as a writer and speaker so that the Panthers would be a little leery about carrying out their contract to kill me.

I told them to wait for a minute and I hurriedly put on some clothes, put my pistol in the closet, and opened the door to the smirking faces of the FBI agents.

They came in, and I got a couple of beers from the refrigerator as we sat down to talk.

I asked them how things were with the Black Panther Party and they told me that Huey Newton was trying to talk the Panthers into running an extortion game on Oakland legitimate businesses, as well as on drug dealers.

I asked how the Panthers were reacting to the book I had written about them (which was getting a lot of publicity).

Kizenski said that FBI informants within the Party were causing a division of thought, because they were saying that I was wrongly expelled, and that my leadership was needed in the Black Panther Party, which, of course, was now nationwide. By this time though, Newton and the Oakland chapter were forgetting about the "revolution" and were concentrating on gang activities. And, of course, Eldridge Cleaver had gone into exile in November of 1968 on the day he was scheduled to return to prison in the shooting where Little Bobby was killed in Oakland. The FBI men merely shrugged when I asked them about Bobby Seale and gave me the impression that Huey was fully in charge of the Panthers now but I knew that, for the most part, the New York Panthers were still loyal to Cleaver.

Then O'Connor got to the point, and told me that their information was that the Mafia had been sending women to me, and wanted me to be a drug runner for them. Kizenski added that the FBI was willing to let me accept the Mafia's offer.

I felt that I was on the spot, so I decided to lie. I said that if the Mafia wanted me to be an interstate drug dealer, I didn't know if I wanted to get involved and would have to think it over because my publisher was talking to me about doing another book.

But, I assured them, I was following their program and I had a young woman named Robin over the night before who I was trying to pimp and get to make deal drugs for me—just as they wanted.

O'Connor told me not to play games with him or thy could bring me in for murder. They still held the 1967 Hunters Point murder of the two Housing Authority policemen, following the shooting and arrest of Huey, over my head although they knew I really knew nothing about it. They had long threatened to railroad me into prison for conspiracy in the murder, although I was out of state when it happened. Along with physical force, this was one of the ways they made me comply with their orders.

I pleaded with them, saying that I would keep my end of the deal and try to infiltrate the Mafia as a pimp and drug dealer.

They didn't threaten me again, instead as they got up to leave, they told me that they would be checking on me—and to keep in contact (we never used phones because they could be bugged by a third party). Even though my book was now out and I was getting a lot of publicity and attention, my life of paranoia was going to continue.

They finally left. I began to feel a tremendous surge of anger and kicked over some chairs and broke a lamp. People were actually dying because of people like them—and I was tired of my role in this sordid affair.

I decided I would, in the future, lie to them, because I didn't want to take another chance just to have the Mafia out to kill me along with the Panthers. And I could not figure out why they needed or wanted me to run dope for them. There were people who would jump at the chance to make that kind of money. I felt that I was being set up. For what, I didn't know. But with O'Connor and Kizenski, one never did know what was coming down.

I knew I would be taking a chance every day as it was, but I wasn't going to let the FBI set me up again. That is what I thought to myself that morning in June, 1970.

CHAPTER VII

A Black Revolutionary Returns Home

I was introduced to Jay Kennedy, the author of the then bestselling book, *The Chairman* in 1968 by a lover we shared in common, Elaine Brown—a young black woman who was to later become a leader in the Black Panther Party.

I was twenty-eight years old, and Jay Kennedy, who was to become an influential politcal power broker within Establishment politics, was fortyish. In his book he discussed in detail the use of lethal bacteria and germ warfare including Agent Orange, which was used by the Americans in Vietnam. Because of this, many of the black revolutionaries, including myself, thought he was working with the Central Intelligence Agency (CIA).

However, I was now a defector from the Black Panther Party and everybody within the Panthers, and the white radical sympathizers, knew that Jay Kennedy, although he might be CIA, also had a reputation as being a fighting liberal from the McCarthy Era, which was responsible for blacklisting artists and entertainers for alleged Communist Party affiliation.

That time destroyed the careers of many artists and entertainers. But it was also the beginnings of the Jewish liberal political movement's "get tough" stance. And these were the mainstay which usually supplied the thinking and money for many Democratic Party politcal candidates.

I felt that Jay Kennedy was the power behind the throne and could put in a good word for me with key people in domestic and international politics, and help me gain a reputation, which would help in the FBI's plan for me to overthrow the Black Panthr Party leadership of Huey Newton, Bobby Seale, and Eldridge Cleaver.

Kennedy was the "prime mover" of several presidential aspirants from the Democratic pool including Senator Hubert Humphrey, who ran in 1968 against the Republican from California, Richard Nixon. He was truly a powerful man.

However, when I decided to meet with Jay Kennedy I thought I would add some fuel to the fire, because the Panthers' leadership had spread the word within the ranks that I might be an informant. It was during the early days of my defection—in fact my first month.

I then met with my COINTELPRO contacts, agents O'Connor and Kizenski, and they told me that I should talk to Jay Kennedy and it was important that I meet with him. I went through with the plan.

We met in the fall of 1968 in the fashionable Polo Lounge in the Beverly Hills Hotel. It was Jay's treat and the meal was delicious. The conversation was just as good. He covered the issues of the day in Establishment politics. I listened intently.

He told me that he had heard from nationally known black author, James Baldwin, that I was about to write a book about the Panthers and my experiences in the Black Panther Party.

I had told James Baldwin of my plans a few weeks before, when I met with him in his large house in the Hollywood Hills for dinner, which was served by a very good looking young Frenchman who was Baldwin's manservant. It was that evening that James gave me the recommendation to his publisher, Dial Press in New York. I contacted Dial through Ron Hobbs, an agent I had gotten in touch with through a friend, Hattie Gossett, ex-wife of Academy award winning actor Lou Gossett Jr. We ended up signing a contract to do the book on my experiences in the Black Panther Party.

I was not to meet with Kennedy again until the early summer of 1970, when *Picking Up the Gun* had been published and was getting national attention. We met many times in expensive East Manhattan restaurants, and it was always Jay's treat.

Jay Kennedy had gotten in contact with me through Dial Press. He was interested in my political direction. I told him I was now a Pan-Africanist and I believed that blacks in America should return to their ancestral homelands and build Africa into a world power.

He was interested, but wanted me to also write and speak about how the black movement in America should become more of a force inside the Establishment politics of the country.

I was to meet his wife later, a lovely woman, who was a psychiatrist. Jay was the Chairman of the Mental Health Association of America. I met many of his clique, young intellectuals and professionals. Most of them seemed to be Jewish. We would listen for hours as Jay told of his experiences as a manager of black singer Harry Belafonte, and as a political activist in the growing Jewish movement, part and parcel of the liberal American political Establishment.

Jay was charismatic and he convinced me to become a panelist on a public television forum for the PBS national network what was to be a three day presentation. He also convinced me to travel to Africa and write a book about the politics of Africa.

The PBS show was entitled *Dissent in America* and it was held in Hershey, Pennsylvania late that same month. I flew down to Pennsylvania from New York with Kennedy. Hershey is a company town, one of the few left in America. It is the home of the famous chocolate company, which bears its name. When we checked into the modern, spacious motel we, like everbody else, were given a complimentary Hershey chocolate bar.

The next day, I went to the auditorium for the first day of the taping for the show. The auditorium held about a thousand people, and it was packed to capacity.

The first day's three hour forum included Jay Kennedy as Chair; Harold Gibbons, then head of the AFL-CIO; Shana Alexander, then, I think, a observor and political columnist for *Newsweek* magazine, and who was later to become a commentator for television's *60 Minutes*; William Atwood, a former CIA bureau chief and then an editor for *Life* magazine; Haskell Wexler, the filmmaker; Sol Yurik, a radical novelist; a psychiatrist, (whose name escapes me now, though I was a house guest of his); and former California Governor, Edmund 'Pat' Brown, Sr. The Reverend Jesse Jackson had been expected but he cancelled out at the last moment, leaving me the only black panelist!

The panel discussion was sharp and I was relatively quiet the first hour and a half. At the break, Haskell Wexler told me that I should "step it up and say more." I remember I was wearing a khaki brown jacket and blue jeans with boots. When we returned for the second half, I totally dominated the panel discussion.

That evening I had dinner with Jay Kennedy and Pat Brown. The next day, I flew back to New York and my flight companion was one of the Hollingworths Group, owners of the then new black women's magazine *Essence*. He told me that they were selling controlling interest to *Playboy* magazine. It was discouraging news, because blacks seem to own so few media outlets in this country.

When I got back to New York from Hershey, I contacted Shelley. She came by my apartment that night. We went for a walk, so our conversation wouldn't be tapped, and I told her to tell the Mafia that I was still undecided about the drug game. Shelley and I had sex that night, and it was the beginning of the long sexual relationship between us. I hoped that Shelley could get the word to the Mafia without the FBI knowing what I told her; and that the Mafia would cool their interest in me (it would be the second time she would run this message).

That morning, after Shelley and I had breakfast, I flew down to Roanoke to think things over. I went back to my aunt and uncle's house. There, I received a phone call offering me a television appearance on a show in Toronto, Canada. I accepted.

I flew to Toronto within the next three days. The city is very clean and beautiful—and so very spread out that it reminded me of Los Angeles.

I was met by the producers of a national Canadian television show, the theme of which was "guess the occupation of this celebrity?" They told me that I was the third black to be on the prime time television show—the others being black civil rights leaders Dick Gregory and Julian Bond.

We had dinner and then the producers took me to the television station and I was the first guest to face the panel, and the studio audience. The panel asked me questions, and they didn't guess my identity. When the host told them I was an ex-Black Panther Party member and writer, the audience gave me a resounding ovation.

The next morning I did a national Canadian radio talk show. Then I visited my Canadian publisher of my *Picking Up the Gun*. My plane was to leave the next morning. I went to another television station where they interviewed me as a prospective guest, which never materialized.

That night I went to see blues singer Joe Williams at a nightclub. I met a hippie white chick at the club, bought her drinks, then we went to her commune, which was crowded with her commune buddies—male and female. We talked, then found an empty room and had sex.

The next day I was on my way back to Manhattan. That day I talked to my agent, Ron Hobbs, and I found out that my proposal to write the first book on America's black student revolt—about the revolt at San Fernando Valley State College in 1969—had been accepted. I signed the contract that day. I had negotiated the deal myself.

It was late June, 1970, and I hadn't been in Los Angeles

since I'd split from the Black Panther Party in 1968. It was a homecoming, with my parents, James and Geraldine Anthony, and my brothers Willard and Ronald Anthony, and my sister, Dr. Barbara Rhodes. Barbara was then a professor at San Fernando Valley State College and made contact for me with the twenty-one year old black man named Archie Chatman, who was the leader of the black student revolt at San Fernando Valley State, which is now known as California State University, Northridge.

I stayed with my brother, Ronald Anthony; and was to conduct three days of intensive interviews with Archie Chatman. I also interviewed my sister, Barbara Rhodes and my longtime friend and "adopted" sister Rhema Gray, also a professor at San Fernando Valley State, and Art Jones, another activist at the college, After leaving Los Angeless, I would conduct telephone interviews with these four people as I developed my book. I was on the phone with one of the four at least twice a week until the book was completed in September of 1970.

Archie Chatman, Uwezo, and Eddie Dancer, the three principle student leaders in the three-day takeover of the president's office at San Fernando Valley State were pushing the demand of a Pan-Africanist department at the college, and were sentenced to twenty years in the California penitentiary. It was the stiffest penalty ever given student activists in America. Archie Chatman, Uwezo, and Eddie Dancer were out on bail that summer. They later escaped to the socialist island of British Guiana. However, their demands for a Pan-Africanist department were met, and that department still exists today.

Archie Chatman and Art Jones, both ex-football players were very cooperative, as were my sister, Dr. Barbara Rhodes, and Rhema Gray as they filled me in on the objectives of the Pan-African department. It was one of many such departments founded on colleges and universities in the black student revolts of the 1960s and 1970s. The idea for a Pan-African college studies program got it's start off campus at

North Carolina A&T, a black college in Greensboro in 1960.

I had become involved in the black student revolt in 1967, at San Francisco State College where the Black Panther Party aided black activists such as Jimmy Garrett, Jerry Varnado, and George Murphy in organizing a student revolt that made national headlines, and was only put down when police invaded the campus. However, the students got their demand of a Black Studies Department. It was the black campus student revolts in America that was copied by other black student activists across the country.

The book on the revolt at San Fernando Valley State was to be the first book of this genre, as was my book on the Panthers the first of that genre. It was to be my second book, and I titled it, *The Time of the Furnaces: A Case Study of Black Student Revolt.*

The title came from a poem by Cuban revolutionary, Jose Marti. Marti writes: "It is the time of the furnaces, and it is only necessary to see the glow." It truly was the time of the furnaces in America, because not only was there a black movement for civil rights and nationalistic and Communist revolt—but white radicals, mostly students and young people, were revolting against America's involvement in the Vietnam war.

When I left Los Angeles for New York aboard a Boeing 747 Jumbo Jet, I reminisced about my times in the city. I had come to Los Angeles from New York via a five month stay in Roanoke, Virginia, when I was thirteen years old.

I finished Foshay Junior High School in the city, where my most vivid memories were of choir; four or five guys singing the first tenor, second tenor, bass, maybe baritone if a quintet, and lead vocalist. We would practice in the bathroom at school, trying to hit fame and fortune, like other black singing groups across America. I kept this quest to form a singing group, singing in school bathrooms, through high school at Dorsey and San Fernando high schools in Los Angeles. I couldn't sing a lick, but I could dance, so I usually sang background. This quest to become part of a singing group in rhythm and blues was to haunt me throughout my teenage years. Nothing came of it.

I might have been the worst second tenor to ever try to form a singing group in those days—before the sound of Motown. We tried and failed several times to make television shows (in fact, when I was eight years old, I tried as a solo vocalist to make the national television show, the "Ted Mack Amateur Hour," and failed).

However, I was a high school and sandlot athlete—playing football, basketball, track, and baseball. I began to play sandlot athletics at seven years of age in Queens, New York, and played continuously after that.

My high school years, aside from athletics and singing, were mostly uneventful. I had no girlfriends to speak of, and I worked as a nurse's aide in the Veteran's Administration Hospital in the San Fernando Valley from the time I was fifteen years old, for about two years.

My grades were not up to par, so I went to a community college, Los Angeles City College, so that I might raise my grades and go to a four year university. I majored in Journalism, and was a sports editor and jazz columnist for the school newspaper.

I used to go to Los Angeles' top jazz club, the Zebra Lounge. The owner of the nightclub was named George Alford, and he was very good in helping me to get interviews with the jazz musicians playing at the club. The interviews were published in the Los Angeles City College newspaper. George Alford gave me a job as his public relations man for his nightclub and concerts. I would hang out at the club and saw many of the best musicians in the business.

I was a real jazz buff and became friends with Richard Bock, president of World Pacific Jazz, which led to me writing album notes for "The Blues Message," with the Curtis Amy and Paul Bryant jazz quintet. I also played baseball with Dick Bock's company team. While writing jazz, I also was an editor for *Angel City* magazine, with people like Dianne Watson and Bill Greene, who were to become state senators in California politics. I was honored by a local black Los Angeles radio station, on their weekly black history personality profile, as the youngest editor in America. I was nineteen years old (I had published my first article when I was twelve years old about the condition of blacks in Harlem for the Amsterdam News).

From Los Angeles City College, my grades were good enough that I was accepted into the University of Southern California in the fall of 1960. My major was English.

At USC, I became a student leader. I was president of my fraternity, Kappa Alpha Psi, as well as being elected Kappa Playboy of the Year in 1962. Also, I was the first black student body officer in the history of the university. I was Executive Secretary of the Interfraternity Council and a member of the Young Republicans.

After graduation from USC, I left Los Angeles in fall 1963, to go to law school in San Francisco.

CHAPTER VIII

The Panthers, The FBI and The Mafia

I was very enthused about writing the book about black student revolt, when I flew from Los Angeles to New York, because I had become friends with the principles involved. I contacted my agent, Ron Hobbs, and he suggested we hook up at the Kennedy International airport with Jim Haskins, a young black writer who was to go on to prominence as the author of dozens of books. When I arrived they were waiting, and the three of us flew down to Washington, D.C. to see a play by another of Hobbs' clients, Paul Carter Harrison, at Howard University. We took a cab from the airport to the University theater.

As Hobbs, Haskins, and I walked into the theater, I was shocked. Sitting in the last row, about twenty men strong wearing black leather jackets, their insignias blazing, were about a dozen Black Panthers!

I was stunned and turned and told Hobbs and Haskins I was going to the bathroom. The Black Panther Party members had not seen me—they were watching the play.

I went to the bathroom, and locked myself into a stall. I knew the Panthers had a contract to kill me, and I was scared. I had my gun, but I didn't want to have to have a shoot out with them, and especially not at the Howard University theater with all those people there.

I wondered how they'd known I would be there. Or was it just a coincidence that they were there. But why so many?

I knew they had put pressure on Hobbs. Maybe he'd told? Fifteen minutes passed, and Hobbs came in the bathroom calling to me by name. I came out of the stall and quickly, and angrily, accused him of setting me up! He denied it and said I could cool it because the Panthers had left.

Hobbs, Haskins, and I watched the play and then went to a party thrown by the cast. I smoked reefer and danced, and let loose my anxieties. (I love to dance, and it has always calmed my nerves).

The next morning, after staying overnight at a hotel, Haskins, Hobbs, and I went back to New York.

That night Hobbs and I had dinner. It was then that he told me that he and Haskins were into white women. I didn't believe it at first because Hobbs' office was staffed fully by black women—all high yellow—like my soon-to-be wife, Robin Bruce, who was his receptionist.

Hobbs asked me if I'd like to hang out with him and Haskins. I decided to check out their set.

For the next two days the three of us were up for forty-eight hours. Following that Saturday night dinner, we partied until the next Monday morning. We went to Manhattan West Side bars, restaurants, and jazz clubs—drinking and talking. Hobbs and Haskins both talked about how superior white women were to black women. I kept disagreeing.

At about four in the morning that Sunday of the first night of the marathon, we went to Hobbs' spacious double tiered apartment in the Chelsea district with three six packs of beer, and three dozen fried chicken wings from the corner deli. We ate and talked.

That morning about 6 a.m., a well known Texas millionaire, famous for his support of right-wing causes, came by with a woman who was a friend of Hobbs, a late thirtyish white woman, who, Haskins told me later, was Hobbs' girlfriend. I asked him what the Texas millionaire was doing with them. "Who knows," he said. "Maybe they're going to have an orgy." Something about that struck both as being very funny. Two kids walking by gave us the sidewalk to ourselves by stepping out into the street.

"They be smoking on dope," one of them said. That made us laugh harder.

Hobbs came up to Haskins' apartment that afternoon. He told me that he had set up a date with a French Anglo female model for me later in the afternoon because, he said, he thought I should try some of what I'd been missing before I continued to go around putting white women down. I went over to her East Side apartment by cab.

I had nothing against white women, and I had gone to bed with a great many of them during my Panther days, and it had always been a pleasant experience.

In fact, the first white woman I had gone to bed with was the wife of a jazz musician who was very involved in raising money for the Los Angeles chapter of the Black Panther Party.

She would always come to Panther meetings and organized the Los Angeles chapter of the white radical political party, the Peace and Freedom Party, which ran the BPP Party Minister of Information, Eldridge Cleaver, in the presidential election of 1968.

So I was game and looked forward to the date Hobbs had arranged for me with this French model.

When I arrived at her place, she was very cordial. We ate cheese and drank wine. She was in her late twenties and very gregarious. She knew of my background in the Black Panther Party and had a copy of my book, which Hobbs had given her.

She was particularly interested in my views of Franz Fanon and the war in Algeria. I told her that I had read Fanon's three books and that I accepted him as one of my leaders. Also, that I believed as he did that blacks were the victims of racism and class exploitation by the bourgeoisie. In fact this view was counter to the Black Panther Party, which believed that blacks in America and around the world were exclusively the victims of class exploitation.

About the war between France and Algeria, I told her that I had heard about it during my stay in Paris the previous year, and although I loved Paris, I thought the French people were culturally chauvinistic.

She gave me a copy of a book by French political theorist, Regris Debray, and told me it was from this book that the Panthers got the concept of revolution by the lumpen proletariat, or the non-working class. I promised her I would read it and later I did.

I told her I wanted to go to bed with her. We did, and as I did then, and always, because somehow I felt white women were more freakish than black women, I gave her oral sex first. Next we sixty-nined each other. Then I screwed her the natural way.

I showered and dressed. I was about to leave when she told me, "I have some friends who would like to make your book on the Panthers into a movie; you can write the script and play yourself in the movie." I asked for their telephone numbers. She said she would be the contact—because they were Mafioso.

I was stunned. The Mafia was still pursuing me—and sending women at me to lure me in.

I knew Huey Newton and the Party were strong-arming and terrorizing Mafia drug dealers on the West Coast at the time; and the Mafia knew the East Coast Panthers, which looked upon me as a leader. I didn't agree with Newton and the West Coast Panthers' move against the drug dealers. The Mafia knew this through Shelley, Hobbs, and FBI informants who had contact with them.

I told her I would tell Ron Hobbs of my decision. Then, I left.

The next day I called that voluptuous nineteen year old, Robin Bruce. She came by my apartment that night. We drove over to New Jersey in a rented car and bought a large quantity of marijuana.

When we came back, Robin told me that she wanted to move in with me. I told her I would call her ex-boyfriend

Carrol—the dope dealer—and we'd go get her clothes. She'd caught me at the right time, and I agreed to let her stay.

We went to Carrol's apartment and got her clothes. When we got back to my place, Robin told me about Claudia—a friend of her's, about the same age who lived on Manhattan's exclusive Sutter Place—and who was a Mafia call girl. She said she would talk to Claudia about how she became a call girl. For some reason, my FBI shadows kept urging me to get a woman and put her on the streets. I don't think Robin was seriously thinking about doing such a thing herself—and there was no way I could have dealt with that in the first place. But, for whatever reason, she felt we should have some information about being a call girl for the Mafia to feed to my FBI contacts.

I told Robin I was tired of talking about the Mafia and that all I wanted to do was get out of New York and write my second book. That was all I wanted to do at the time.

Robin suggested the New York summer resort town of Sag Harbor, where her mother and stepfather had a summer house. I told her we should go there and I would rent a motel.

We left for Sag Harbor the next morning. I was to fall in love with the place in the Hamptons, where I was to stay through July and August of 1970. This was the home of high society—both black and white.

It was to be a summer of fun on that small tip of Long Island. Robin and I would bicycle ten miles to our favorite beach spot just to swim and relax. I would be writing all the while. Sometimes we would ride horses there.

Nights were spent talking after returning from dinner. In the eight months I lived with her, we ate out every meal—she would never cook.

Robin was also a drugger and we smoked reefer every day we were in Sag Harbor.

She was fascinated by my experiences in the Panther movement, and so was her older brother David (he was twenty one years old). As a matter of fact, they kept talking to me about starting a new terrorist black movement organization.

Robin became pregnant with my child during that summer. I also finished my second book, *Time of the Furnaces*.

I had been contacting O'Connor and Kizenski at the FBI by registered mail in D.C. I told them I was trying to build my image as a revolutionary writer, then lied by saying that I was grooming Robin to be a call girl because she had some Mafia drug contacts that I was cultivating.

I wrote O'Connor and Kizenski that as soon as I finished this book, I would be in motion on the call girl and drug scene with Robin. This gave the impression that I could easily infiltrate the Mafia.

Back in Manhattan in September, 1970 with the book at the publishers, my life with Robin began to change. Robin was miserable in the morning, having morning sickness and pains from her pregnancy.

It was distressing for her. We tried to enjoy ourselves; we would rent bicycles and go through Central Park and the midtown area. We did have some fun.

Because we ate out so often, several of the restaurants and bars in Harlem knew us by name: Small's Paradise, Obie's, Wells', Frank's, and Boomer's in the Chelsea District, where my well-built, tall, dark, and handsome friend Gene Lewis was now maitre'd.

We would visit Robin's friends, too: Janice, who was married to Harry; Shyleen and Glen; and Deniece, who was to marry Curtis, then her boyfriend. We would toot coke and smoke reefer and talk.

It was not long after we returned to the city, in late September of 1970, that I got a call from my agent. Woodie King, who was the premier black stage producer in New York, wanted to talk to me about my two one act plays.

I knew of King's reputation as a stage producer—and he has continued to be the premier black stage producer—not only in New York, but in the entire country during the 1970s and 1980s.

I went over to his apartment on Riverside Drive in Midtown Manhattan. Robin came with me. We went out to the popular Mikell's restaurant and Woodie said he wanted to produce the plays, *The Misjudgement*, the story about a police informer inside the Black Panther Party; and *Charlie Still Can't Win No Wars on the Ground*, the dark comedy about a Panther and a Black Muslim arguing over the relevance of America's first flight to the moon, which I'd written that night back in the winter while visiting in Roanoke.

Woodie King said he would produce the two one act plays— as *Two Plays by Earl Anthony*—at his theater, the New Federal Theater.

Woodie was friendly, and throughout the conversation that night and through our long friendship, I would come to understand that he has a profound understanding of black American culture and politics, gained by his experience and reading.

The New Federal Theater was the revival of the Federal Theater, founded by famous Anglo actor, Orson Welles who had been one of the producers of Richard Wright's *Native Son*. I was happy to be doing plays for Woodie King's New Federal Theater. The plays were scheduled for February, 1971.

I got a job as a consultant for the New York City Board of Education in the Bronx ghetto district. My job was handling special programs in the district (I scheduled people such as black singer Lou Rawls; and concerts with black dance and acting troops, all of which were successful.)

While working that job, I was contacted again, in October, by O'Connor and Kizenski. They were sitting outside my office building in a car waiting for me.

Usually there was tension in our conversation, but they seemed pleasantly surprised that I was making a name for myself as a writer. It was their feeling, confirmed, they said, by FBI informants inside the Black Panther Party, that my expulsion had caused resentment in most circles; and that there was serious internal conflict within the Party.

They seemed a little impatient that I had not started working drugs and using Robin as a prostitute, because it was their feeling that the Panthers were going to become a strictly drug gang.

Then they gave me a time schedule. They would see me in March, 1971, after my publishing date and the production of my plays. By that time they wanted me to be drug dealing and also to have Robin set up as a call girl.

I was to quit the consultant job in February, 1971, when I went to Africa—even though I was making great money. However, it was my intention to take Robin and run from the FBI.

While working as a consultant for the Board, I began a love affair with a black school teacher named Janet. It wasn't long before Robin began to sense that I was having an affair. It made her angry, starting many of our arguments.

The love affair with Janet continued. We would check into midtown hotels many days after she had finished teaching at her school.

The arguments with Robin continued and some nights I would leave the apartment angry and go to Times Square, and into the topless bars to catch a show with the naked girls; and often I would pick up a black prostitute. I always could go for a little sleaze.

Robin's sickness continued; she'd throw up blood in the morning. And, although she was angry about the affair, she was passionate and we continued to make love. I guess I was on an ego trip with Janet and the prostitute scene.

To ease Robin's pain I catered to her. Each weekend we would check into a different large midtown hotel and spend the time like the rich, ordering room service meals and spending "time away from the office."

I was putting double duty on my credit cards, using them to entertain both Robin and Janet; but then, I had no concept of credit or money.

Robin went into the hospital in November, 1970, and had to have an abortion after being diagnosed as having a tubular pregnancy, a life-threatening condition.

She was depressed afterwards and to help her recover, we decided to go to Jamaica. I got the time off from my Board job and we left.

I love the Caribbean, but prior to going there with Robin, had only visited there alone. Later, I would return with my second wife, Gayle Smallwood-Shields.

It was relaxing the week we spent in Jamaica; relaxing from the ordeal of the abortion. We stayed in a villa hotel in Montego Bay, a notorious tourist trap.

In the morning, after a breakfast of fresh fish and fruit, we would head out to the beach, with its white sand and would swim in the calm, crystal-clear ocean water.

Robin and I ate the exotic foods; I picked up a taste for curried chicken, fish, and beef. We rode horses, and there was one ride I will always remember. It was past an bauxite plant—bauxite is the principal resource in Jamaica—and the tour guide told me that Jamaicans who worked in the plant industry made a little more than two-thousand dollar a year, and were considered elitist. That was because the average Jamaican family in 1970 made only three-hundred dollars a year.

Robin and I did some sight seeing around the island of Jamaica, but we did no nightlife. We went to bed early, after enjoying our evening drinks following dinner. It was quiet and peaceful.

Back in New York from Jamaica, I contacted Woodie King about the plays of mine he was to do, and he told me about a book deal that he had with New American Library to edit anthologies about the black experience in America. I asked Woodie if I could co-edit an anthology with him, and he agreed.

It was to be my third book—the anthology I named *Black Poets and Prophets*. It consisted of essays by Stokely Carmichael, Eldridge Cleaver, Ron Karenga, LeRoi Jones, Woodie King, myself, and others.

I wrote for the permissions to use these easays written by these black personalities. Robin and I went to Washington, D.C., and even made a search of Newark trying to contact the evasive Stokely Carmichael, and the mercurial LeRoi

Jones a.k.a. Imamu Baraka, respectively.

It took me about three weeks to pull the book together, and present it to King so that he would be able to submit it to the publisher. It was December, 1970, and the book was published in February, 1971.

After its completion, Robin asked if we could go to the Carribean again. I consented, although I was in over my head, financially. She wanted to go to Antigua because she had fond memories of being there with her mother and stepfather.

We left for the Islands in early December on a bitter cold day. It was to be a pleasurable week of swimming, tanning, and horseback riding on the beautiful, lazy shores.

During that week I mulled over an idea for a fourth book.

When we got back to the States, I called my editor at Dial Press, Don Hutton, and asked him if I could write a pitch for a book idea about Africa. He consented and within the week I met with him. He took me to an exclusive French restaurant off Third Avenue in the midtown area (you were supposed to have a tie on; I didn't and was somewhat embarrassed, but the maitre'd was happy to lend me one).

I pitched the book on the direction of African politics; my working title was *The African Question*. Hutton, a midthirties Anglo, man was a senior editor at Dial Press. He liked the idea and we roughly ironed out the details for a book contract on the politics of Africa over the three hour lunch.

We were to sign the contract within the next week. I was also to fire my agent, Ron Hobbs, because I had worked out the last three deals by myself and I suspected him of trying to set me up with the Black Panther Party months earlier. I didn't like his lack of respect for black women, and all and all, that was enough to let him go.

I was contacted in December, 1970—through Dial, by the then largest public speaking bureau—the American Program Bureau. They had four universities that wanted me to speak through January of 1971.

After Chrismas and New Year's, which I spent with my family in Los Angeles and Roanoke (Robin was with her family in Chicago), I came back to New York to begin my lecture tour. I was paid one-thousand dollars a speech, with accommodations, food, and travel paid by the hosting university—usually the black student union of the respective college.

This time, Robin was with me. She really enjoyed being on tour with me, through upstate New York, Minnesota, Wisconsin, and Ohio.

I would explain the concept of Black Power and the Black Panther Party principles. Then I called for black Americans to go to Africa to help them improve life there. The justification for this was that blacks in America are African-Americans.

This four city, four university speaking tour was covered by the local newspapers at each stop. And, I was interviewed several times by local television stations.

In 1981 I was to find out that the FBI was also covering the tour, recording my speeches (this is part of the 666 page file they have about me that I was later to receive a copy of).

February was to be a good month for me. *Time of the Furnace: Case Study for Black Student Revolt*, was published in hardback and also softcover, receiving many national reviews. Also, Woodie King and the New Federal Theater did *Two Plays by Earl Anthony*. My career seemed to be at a new high. Robin and I went to see my plays and they were so popular that I remember there was one black youth who could remember every line of *Charlie Still Can't Win No Wars on the Ground*, and still laugh out loud. In the same month a book, which included two essays that I edited—*Black Poets and Prophets*—was published.

I had become, finally, an established black leader, through my writings and experiences, and mostly through my writing about my personal experience.

Later that month, Robin Bruce, formally became my wife, Robin Anthony. It was a bitter-sweet experience. The night before our marriage and reception was to take place at the exclusive Warwick Hotel (attended by over a thousand people) I slapped her around because of an argument.

A couple of weeks after the wedding, Robin and I went to Los Angeles to visit my family.

From Los Angeles I went alone to Oklahoma to speak at the State University. When I returned, Robin greeted me at the airport. But an argument ensued when she said she "smelled another woman on me." I denied it.

To please her about the situation, I decided to take her to San Francisco. We stayed at the fashionable Miyako Hotel. But the argument continued so I went out the first night and found a prostitute. Robin left me that night saying she was going to Denver to stay with her friend, Shyleen.

Alone, I returned to New York. I was supposed to meet O'Connor and Kizenski upon my arrival.

But after considering it, I decided I was fed up and within a week I was on my way to London—only a stop over—then on my way to Africa. I was going to relocate permanately there. I felt I had gotten in too deep being an informant, and that this self-imposed exile was my only way out. I had hopes that Robin would join me there.

Chapter IX

My African Conversion

When I came back from Los Angeles to New York, I landed at JFK and went directly to the TWA desk to make my reservation for the trip to Africa. It was late February, 1971.

There was also other plane reservations to make; I intended to make a quick trip to Denver to pick up Robin. My plan, at the time, was to take her to Africa with me, although I hadn't seriously discussed it with her and she had not said she would go. But I was being fueled by emotion, not logic.

Although I had over extended my credit, all the air charges went through, or so it seemed. Then the woman at the counter said there would be a short delay. I don't know why, but I panicked and ran. Of course I was stopped by airport police. I was later charged with credit card fraud.

I was taken to the airport police station first, and put into a cell for a few hours, while the usual police and FBI check was run on me. Then I was transported to the notorious Manhattan Tombs jail. I was put into the maximum security section, where I ended up in a tiny cell with a top and lower bunk, open toilet, and barely room to turn around.

My cellmate was a black man in his early thirties, who was to stand trial for murder. I learned he had been in the Tombs for close to a year, which was dead time in that it would not count against his prison sentence by the judge—when and if he was convicted.

He was a bitter man. And, as he said, "I'm a tough guy—penitentiary time ain't nothing for me."

After a couple of hours in the cell, and the usual jail talk ("What are you in for?" and so forth) my cellmate learned my name and, yes, I was the same Earl Anthony who had been a member of the Black Panthers and written the book. My cellmate (I've forgotten his name) said that he'd read *Picking Up The Gun*. From the detail that he recalled, I suspected he actually had. And since I could fill him in where his memory was spotty, I think he finally became convinced that I really was "that Earl Anthony." I, at his prodding, ended up telling about being an ex-Panther Party Deputy Minister of Information, and about the duties that went with the title. Soon, while I was talking, I noticed that the people in the adjoining cells had stopped talking. A hush had fallen over the entire cell block, and I realized they were listening to me.

It turned out that what I was saying was going over big among jail inmates because the Panther Party was composed mostly of street gang members and ex-penitentiary inmates. And the Panthers had earned their reputation among this element in confrontations with the police, most of them ending in death for the Panthers. Actually, I was the first bourgeois memeber of the Black Panther Party, as pointed out by founder Huey Newton in one of his books, *Revolutionary Suicide*.

A few hours after I had been locked down, I went in front of the lineup, and then taken back to my cell. In my FBI files this entire incident is reported and it is explained that I was being investigated for murder, bank robbery, and bank fraud (in the lineup); and that I was armed and extremely dangerous. My FBI informant activities were entirely blacked out.

I was guilty of nothing. I put in a call to Robin's mother—Dessie Bruce—and asked her to bail me out.

The next day I was told that I was being released. My

cellmate asked me, rather intimidatingly, to deliver a note to one of his friends in town. He told me to stick the note up my ass, so the jail guards wouldn't find it. And when I got out, to shit and the note would come out.

I did as he told, but when I was released an hour later, the guards, during their skin search of me, made me shit and they found the note. They still released me.

A couple of days later my court date was set for August, 1971. I paid a lawyer, and gave him a certified check for twenty-three thousand dollars to pay off my creditors.

That night I caught the first flight I could to Africa—with a stopover in London. It was now March, 1971, and I had just turned thirty-one years old.

I flew first class to London, and in the cabin with me was the famous female white radical from Ireland, Bernadette Devlin, a newly elected member of Parliament.

When we landed in London the next day, Bernadette and I posed together for photographs for the newspapers of England and Ireland.

I had lived for a short time in London a year or so earlier, and knew the city well. I took one of the large European cabs, with two sets of seats in them, to the Hilton where I was to stay for four days.

I talked to my London agent, a young white woman named Cheryl, the first day I got in, about a second book about Africa. I would be a specialized book on African liberation struggles. It would be different from the book on African policy, which would include the subjects of independent African nations and Pan-Africanism. The second book—for which I had written a proposal—would be about guerrilla movments in Africa. All of these movements, or at least nearly all, were Socialist.

Cheryl, who had been my agent since my first stay in London in 1969, arranged to introduce me to Margaret Busby the co-owner of the publishing house of Allison-Busby.

She was accompanied by a young white man named Allison. Margaret was a beautiful African woman from Ghana, and

I was very impressed by her.

Margaret and I made the rounds of the city pubs, drinking, eating, and talking about Africa. I believe she was caught up in my enthusiasm, because on the fourth day—the day I was to leave for Lagos, Nigeria—we signed a contract for the book.

Then we went to my hotel room, ordered up dinner and drinks, and end up making a party of our celebration.

She went to the airport to see me off. I had my passport but not a visa for Africa. Margaret thought I was crazy not to stay a day more in London, and get my visa. But I was so caught up in the after glow of sex—and following my destiny—that I just didn't do it. I think Margaret thought I was childlike in my behavior, but I only knew I was committed to my cause.

I flew out that night on BOAC airlines on my way to Nigeria. I flew first class and the only black person in the same area was the first wife of Sidney Poitier—I didn't know who she was until we landed.

I also discovered later that she and two white associates were going to Africa to explore plans to open a hotel. I was to meet them, and discuss each of our reasons for being in Nigeria once the plane landed, while waiting in the VIP section of the airport.

When the plane landed I was one of the first people off and when I got to the ground I fell to one knee and kissed it. I was finally in Africa—the homeland—a fulfillment of a dream.

There was an excitement at the airport. A Nigerian Army rifle squad, in formation, was firing a twenty-one gun salute. The young Nigerian man carrying my bags told me what it was all about. The American civil rights leader Whitney Young, head of the Urban League, had drowned the day before in the deep choppy Atlantic off the coast of Lagos.

Air Force General B.O. Davis had flown to Lagos to take Whitney Young's body back to the States. Whitney Young and other civil rights leaders, including the Reverend Jesse

Jackson were there that week for a Pan-African business conference.

When I checked in at customs at the airport, the Nigerian customs official who I dealt with said I couldn't go through because I didn't have a visa.

The BOAC pilot behind me in line whispered to me, "Bribe him, they'll take it."

I offered a bribe to the man. Fifty American dollars. He told me to step to the side. A few minutes later he told me, "It will take five-hundred dollars for me to get you a visa."

I told him I would give him one-hundred dollars, and he could check my credentials with Julia Herve, with whom I stayed in Paris a few years before, and who was then with the Ministry of Information in Lagos.

I also told him to check with Donald Smith who was with an American research group in Lagos. He was a family friend of Robin's and was expecting my visit.

The customs official made the calls to Donald and Julia, while I returned to the VIP lounge in the airport to wait.

Donald, a middle aged light complexioned man, came to get me at the airport. I paid the Nigerian official one-hundred dollars, and he gave me a Nigerian visa, and let me enter the country.

Once I was out of the airport proper, I found that the sun in Nigeria is scorching. And like everywhere I went in Lagos, there were hundreds of hustlers around the airport—cab drivers, luggage men, and tour guides.

As we drove into Lagos proper, I saw military truck convoys with armed soldiers everywhere. The Nigerian civil war had not ended too long before. Donald told me that I should watch out for the military men, for they had a reputation of terrorizing the people for profit; and particularly as had a specialized visa as a journalist. It seemed that the media was not very popular with the military in Nigeria, or at least not in Lagos.

I was to stay in Lagos for a week. It is an exciting city. The Nigerians were out in the city's streets in droves both day and night, and the beer gardens were packed all the time.

I stayed at Donald's large Victorian-style house, a reminder of the English colonial period in Nigeria. Donald introduced me to Will Petty, a tall, lean man about my age, who was head of the U.S. Information Agency in Nigeria.

I spent time touring the city and talking to Petty, who was a Vietnam War veteran, and Will set up an interview for me for the Lagos Times—Nigeria's largest newspaper.

The interview came out on my third day, and it was the major story on the front page of the Sunday paper. It was titled: "Black Panther Comes Home to Africa to Pick Up the Gun." It had a picture of me; information about my educational background and that the fact that now I had committed myself to live in Africa in the country of Tanzania. At that time, I intended to walk out on the credit card fraud charge as well as the FBI.

The story in the paper was, I was to learn later, reprinted in my FBI file. I was later to disover that I had even been followed to Africa.

After the front page story, I was known by Nigerians all over the city who would approach me on the street. I would also be approached by young men in the bars where I would be drinking beer. I had become quite a celebrity in Lagos.

It was my next to the last day in Lagos. I had been invited to dinner at the home of US Information Agency bureau chief Will Petty and his wife.

There were two other people as guests at the villa of the Pettys: an African marketplace woman, and a large black man who appeared to be in his early thirties named Gene, who Will introduced as a reporter for the New York *Times*.

I gave copies of my three recently published books to everyone in the room. Aside from the small talk, and talk of African culture, the others wanted to know about black Americans like Huey Newton, Stokely Carmichael, Eldridge Cleaver, and H. Rap Brown—and how the black American movement was doing. I brought them up to date on these matters.

Gene said he wanted to do an interview with me, and we made an appointment to meet at a hotel bar the next afternoon.

Gene and I met the next day as planned. As I entered the hotel, I met Gil Hernandez, a major officer in the African liberation group from Guinea-Bissau, who was headquartered in Egypt.

Gene and I had drinks, and he inquired about my future plans. I told him that I planned to live in Africa. I was going to write two books on Africa that I had contracted for; one on African politics in independent African countries, and the other on Socialist African liberation movements which were trying to win independence for the African nations.

I told Gene that Will Petty had given me a US Information Agency contact in Nairobi, Kenya, and that I was going there next. From there I intended to go to Lusaka, Zambia, because most African liberation groups were headquartered there; and then to what most black America Pan-Africanists felt was Utopia, the Socialist country of Tanzania. I was to set up my base of operations in Dar es Salaam, Tanzania.

Gene said he would hook up with me again in Tanzania, and would do a major interview with me, but wanted to introduce me to an important African liberation leader from Zaire. He warned me that the man wanted to recruit me as a leader for African liberation movements.

He was living at the hotel and Gene took me to his room to introduce me to Roberto, and then left the two of us together. Gene went over my background with Roberto, but it was apparent that he already knew all about me. They also talked about my reason for being in Africa. It ws obvious that I had been highly recommended to Roberto, as a future Pan-Africanist leader.

When Gene left and we were alone, Roberto grabbed the reins of the conversation and began by telling me that the liberation struggles in the southern countries of Africa—meaning Rhodesia (now Zimbabwe), Mozambique, Southwest

Africa (now Naimbia), Angola, South Africa, as well as in Guinea-Bissau in West Africa, were being fought militarily and politically by liberation organizations that were opposed to each other. And although all of them were for the same goal, independence and black African rule, he pointed out that only one side could win the struggle eventually and as long as you had these various groups fighting each other, expending resources, nothing was going to change.

I told him I knew this, and that I wanted to write and interview only Socialist groups who were engaged in the struggle for the liberation of Africa.

Roberto told me that as an African-American, and a well known writer and speaker from the movement for liberation in America, I could either have a great impact—or be used as a pawn by the Socialists to promote their groups in Southern Africa.

Roberto asked me whether I wanted to be a leader in African liberation movements. I answered that I was not an African national of any particular country but wanted to live on the African continent. And yes I would like to be a political and military leader of the struggles in Africa.

Roberto stressed that I was an African-American, but everywhere in Africa our black movement in America was talked about and highly regarded. He suggested that I talk to all the leaders in the movement in Africa, making friends with as many of them as possible. Then he stressed that I should realize that America, like China and Russia, also give support to African liberation struggles for independence.

Roberto said that he was supported by the United States—and specifically, the CIA. He added that if I was interested, he would give me contacts to the CIA supported liberation groups in Lusaka, Zambia.

I hedged. He went to the closet and brought out an attache case. He said there were ten-thousand Nigerian dollars in it. He wanted to give it to me as partial payment, with ten more thousand to come, if I would write my two books about Africa in a way that was partial to the American backed liberation groups and the indepedent nations. He also suggested I speak to and try to recruit black youths to come to Africa to train and fight with the CIA-backed African liberation groups. Years later, when I received my CIA file of 102 pages, there was nothing about the Nigerian escapade. It would have been reported through the Central Intelligence Agency Operations division, and while I also had other dealings with them, none of it was in the file I obtained from them.

Roberto was persuasive. I decided to take the money and change directions, supporting American-backed liberation groups instead of the Socialists, as I had promised. I also accepted his contacts in Zambia. That night I was on my way from Lagos, Nigeria in West Africa to Nairobi, Kenya, in East Africa.

I flew Ethiopian Airlines to Nairobi. Again I was seeing an excellent example of skilled blacks—who had been trained in hotels and airline operations by Americans or European whites. It was a class act. I was to also to learn this about the construction of the buildings, the operation of the hospitals—everything. It was clear that whatever development there had been in Africa was due to the white man and woman. And, as I was to later discover, this was the case throughout the continent, whether the countries were in the Capitalist or Socialist camp.

When I arrived in Nairobi, I went to the American Hilton. I was to be there three weeks. The climate was tropical, and cooler than Lagos. And, like Nigeria, it was in the American camp, being aided by the government of United States—and formerly supported by England.

The first day I was in Nairobi, which was ruled by Prime Minister, Jomo Keyatta, I contacted in person (by going to her office) an attractive middle aged black woman named Doris, who headed the US Information Agency in Kenya. We had a cordial conversation about black Americans and African politics at an East Indian restaurant.

I told her of meeting the African liberation leader, Roberto, and of his convincing me to change my stance to support American-supported African liberation groups and independent nations. She congratulated me on my new-found political development and maturity.

The next day I saw her at her office. Doris told me that she had set up a thirty minute interview for me on national Kenya television. It was to be a live telecast, and to take place at 6 p.m. the next day in the Nairobi television facilities.

I thanked her for the chance to get exposure for my views.

I went to a disco that afternoon, frequented mostly by European tourists and Africans; and that night I went to a nightclub on the outskirts of the city, where the customers were all Africans, save me.

The music at the club was African, but similar to black American music. I danced and drank, and left with a young African woman.

I went to a small shack in a village outside of Nairobi. We were driven there in a '71 Peugeot, driven by the African guide I had hired.

The driver waited and slept outside, while we went into the Kenyan woman's house, and we had straight sex (African women, at least at that time, didn't do different sexual positions, or oral sex).

The next day, after my first sexual experience with an African woman, and my fourth day in the country, I returned to the hotel for a rooftop swim, and then a countryside drive.

After dinner in one of Nairobi's many fine restaurants, I went to the very modern national television station to be interviewed.

I was seated facing two Kenyans, both of whom appeared to be in their early thirties and dressed in business suits. I wore a khaki bush jacket, slacks and boots. The opening remarks were about my background and credentials as an author. They went on to state that now I was in Africa to establish a base of opperation.

I then stated how Pan-Africanism was the philosophy of the 1970s amongst black American activists, and how I felt they would come around to giving any knowledge and experiences they had to Africa.

Then the questioning began by the pair—who were basically very skeptical, it seemed toward me and what I had to say. Once one of them said, "Kwame Nkrumah, the great African leader, and Former Prime Minister of Ghana, couldn't spread Pan-Africanism in Africa, so why do you feel you can what such a man as Nkrumah could not accomplish?"

I replied, telling him: "It was not the man, but the times that would dictate that Pan-Africanism be spread across the continent of Africa. Kwame Nkrumah was before his time."

After the interview I went to dinner with Doris of USIA, and she told me that she tought the interview went smoothly.

Three weeks later I left Nairobi in an excellent mood and flew Zambian Airways to Lusaka, the next leg on my African adventure. I loved the exotic African food and female African stewardesses on the flight.

When I landed I took a taxicab through the dark tropical contryside—running over the largest snake I have ever seen—into the modern city of Lusaka, Zambia, and to the exclusive Intercontinental Hotel.

I went down to the bar that night, and ran into a contingent of black men from New York and Los Angeles who were in Africa on business deals. I ate and drank with them that night, and every night at the hotel, during the three weeks I was to be in Lusaka. Eventually I began to dislike them because of their crude and haughty attitude and actions toward the native Africans they met.

The morning after my arrival, I went to what was called "Liberation Village" on the outskirts of the city. This was an enclosed compound of offices representing all liberation groups from South Africa, Angola, Mozambique, Zimbabwe (South Rhodesia), and Southwest Africa (Naimbia). The groups were supported by Russia, China, and the United States. My first meeting was with the leader of the liberation group PAC, supported in their guerrilla warfare struggle in South Africa by China.

I had long conversation with an intelligent man named Cliff who was the head of PAC. That night he invited me to dinner with the Chinese ambassador and his wife, and Cliff's wife. I accepted.

Later in the evening, Cliff and his wife picked me up at the hotel and we went to the plush home of the Chinese Ambassador to Zambia. The Chinese food was delicious, and the conversation was great.

One thing the ambassador told me, among other things, was that there are over one-hundred tribes, with different language dialects in China, which made it difficult for Chairman Mao to centralize power there.

I was to go to Liberation Village each day of the three weeks that I was in Lusaka.

One day, as I entered Liberation Village, I heard a loud explosion. People emptied out of the bungalow offices.

The explosion had come from the ZANU office. It had killed the liberation leader of ZANU. The liberation leaders at the scene blamed the CIA, after discovering the explosion was caused by a paper bomb which had been sent through the mail in a box that ignited when opened.

After three weeks in Lusaka, Zambia I left, and flew to my final destination, Dar es Salaam in Tanzania. I was to stay at the modern Kilimanjaro Hotel for the three months that I was in the city. Here, as elsewhere in Africa where I visited social life among the business and political African elite, and tourist, was centered in the hotels, usually in the restaurants or bars.

My first day in Tanzania I ran into Fred Brooks and Charlie Cobb, from the black power organization, SNCC. They told me that they were living in Tanzania, and had been recruiting black American professionals such as schoolteachers, and putting them under contract to come to Africa and work.

I was also introduced during my stay to black church officials Yenwith Whitney and Leon Modeste, who, through the United Presbyterian and United Methodist churches, were financing the black programs in Tanzania.

My best friend in Tanzania was John Manning from the Malcolm X University, a community school teaching black politics in Lawrence, Kansas. Manning and two or three other Kansas blacks had a farm which raised chickens in Tanzania which was also financed by the Presbyterian and Methodist churches.

I was with John Manning every day in Tanzania, getting together early in the morning at the hotel. We would go to the village, where we would drink beer and smoke marijuana with the people.

We also visited work places, as John showed me the progress Tanzanian Prime Minister Julius Nyerere was making in Socialism.

My nights were mostly spent with a young brown-skinned American black woman whom I had met a few days after I arrived.

We enjoyed dinners at the rooftop restarant of the Kilimanjaro Hotel, and had conversation about the future of Africa. She was in Africa to stay, or so she said.

I had tired of womanizing for the moment, but in Stephanie—that was her name—I was able to get my fill of lovemaking. She had the same excellent qualities, sensually, that I have found in all black women, American, Caribbean, and African.

Stephanie had a round ass and hairy crotch—and loved sex.

But having Stephanie could not ease my hurt from not being with my wife, Robin.

I had started writing Robin when I was in Nigeria, and continued in Kenya and Zambia. But I didn't receive any return letters.

When I got to Dar es Salaam, I started calling her on the phone. She said she didn't write back because I was moving from place to place too quickly.

I told her that I loved her, and wanted her to come live with me in Africa. She assured me that she loved me as well, but did not want to live in Tanzania.

I was too ashamed to tell her about my involvement with the FBI as an informant; and that I was trying to avoid the FBI, and that I had accepted money to live on from a CIA operative, Roberto from Zaire.

I literally begged Robin to come live with me in Africa, but she was steadfast in wanting me to come back to the States.

CHAPTER X

The Real Streets of San Francisco

After five months in Africa, I decided to leave, to go back to New York to stand trial on the credit charge fraud I was accused of, and to see Robin.

I called the CIA-supported liberation leader Roberto in Zaire, and told him that I would slant both of my books on Africa to support American groups and independent nations. I also told him that in my speeches I would also support the American side in Africa, and would try to recruit groups of young black Americans to follow me back to Africa when I returned.

My parents, James and Geraldine Anthony, were vacationing in Tanzania, and I caught a TWA flight back to New York with them.

It was the beginning of August, 1971. When I finally got to my apartment, I called Robin in Denver.

She said she was fine, that everything was okay with her. I asked her to come to New York, and told her that I wanted her to go back to Africa with me after my trial, which was due to begin in two days.

I wired her money for a ticket, and the next day I met her at JFK International. We went to her mother's apartment (her mother and family were out at their summer home in Sag Harbor, Long Island).

We bought a bottle of cognac, our favorite drink, and began to talk. I told her of my experiences in Africa, being careful not to mention the womanizing. She told me she had joined a poetry group in Denver and that she found it very exciting.She also mentioned several times how much she liked the city

I was getting high on the cognac, and so was she, and she finally told me, cautiously: "I am in love with somebody else. His name is Melvin Brisco and he lives in Denver."

I went into a blind rage and began beating her in the body with karate chops. This went on for what seemed like an hour, until she passed out. Later, she told me that I had fractured her ribs.

When she regained consciousness we had sex; then I took her to the airport for her flight back to Denver. I knew I had lost her. I was angry that I had gotten drunk and treated her the way I had. Years later, when I went through therapy, I was finally made to realize that every time I had become violent with a woman it was after I had been drinking.

I went to trial a day later, and the fraud case was dropped because my lawyer had paid off my creditors with money I'd sent him.

I met that afternoon with Woodie King. We'd stopped by a bookstore that specialized in black material and were talking when I told him I was leaving New York. He tried to convice me to stay.

That evening I flew from New York to San Francisco. I was heartbroken over having lost Robin.

I checked into the Hilton in downtown San Francisco. I was there only a few hours when there was a knock at the door. I answered and there stood my FBI shadows, O'Connor and Kizenski, with the familiar arrogant expressions on their faces.

I let them in, hoping they knew about the deal I had made with Roberto and the CIA, which I told them all about once they were in the room.

The agents said they were going to take me in for conpiracy

to murder because I had not been cooperating with them, had not been following their orders. I told them I was going to see some reporters because my civil rights were being violated.

When I said that, Kinzenski hit me hard in the jaw, knocking me to the bed. I screamed that I wanted out; and that I was now working with the CIA.

O'Connor called me a liar. Then he pulled his gun and threatened to kill me. I still pleaded that I wanted out.

O'Connor put the gun to the temple of my head, and Kizenski took three or four solid hits to my mouth and jaw until I was unconscious.

They were gone when I regained consciousness.

I checked out of the hotel that evening and went over to the home of Alonzo X, my friend who was a renegade member of the Black Muslims in America, and one of the men who had rescued me when the Panthers put me under house arrest.

I was to stay with him and his wife, Carmelita, in a large apartment, which was frequented by dozens of black people, both Muslims and non-Muslims. I was comfortable around the Black Muslims. Although I had joined the Muslims in 1964, becoming Earl X, I never became an active member. However, I did live a considerable amount of time with the group that included Alonzo X.

I had been staying at Alonzo's only two days when, as I was returning home to the apartment one night, I saw a late model car in front of the building. I felt as if I'd been punched in the guts when I saw it was O'Connor and Kizenski. They got out of the car as I walked over. There was nothing else I could do but confront them.

Then they asked met to get in the back seat, which I did. They drove me out to the beach, taking their time about it. I really didn't know what was up and was a little bit afraid because of the last time. However, during the ride they apologized for the way they'd treated me, and said they had checked out my CIA story and found it to be true.

Once we got to the beach, O'Connor said they had twenty pounds of high grade marijuana, and they knew, from the last time I lived with Alonzo in 1968, that he and several of his Muslin friends were small time gangsters.

O'Connor and Kizenski wanted me to organize a marijuana distribution ring. I would get the dope from them, meeting them once a week at the Fairmont Hotel in downtown San Francisco. I would get the marijuana in suitcases, which I'd put in my rented car, and be the distributor for our Muslim ring.

O'Connor and Kizenski said the FBI informants had spread the word inside the Black Panther Party that I was selling marijuana inter-state for the Mafia through my renegade Muslims friends. The Black Panther Party, which was trying to control drugs in northern California, were leery about attacking anybody affiliated with the Nation of Islam. According to these FBI agents, the word had been put out to leave me alone.

I decided I would accept the FBI deal because I was afraid of the repercussions that would probably come my way if I did not. And, at least, I would have some money in my pocket.

When I brought the twenty pounds of dope to Alonzo, he quickly agreed to organize a few Muslim brothers.

The operation was immediately successful and we were to grow to where we were bringing in five to ten thousand dollars a week from the streets. And we never got busted, although some of the sellers on the street were constantly getting arrested. But then, O'Connor and Kizenski said that they had notified San Francisco police intelligence that we were dealing marijuana as an FBI sting to start warfare between the Black Panther Party and a fringe group of non-active, gangster Muslims.

We were called the "gang of five renegade Muslims": Alonzo X, James X, Hakim, Ali, and myself, Earl X. And we were to deal twenty to forty pounds of marijuana a week from 1971 to 1974, when I suffered a major nervous breakdown, triggered by which I am convinced to this day was a hallucinogenic drug deliberately given to me by a government agency.

We were to lose Alonzo X in 1972 because he went to jail for counterfeit, another gangster hustle he was into. But we always split the five to ten thousand a week evenly among the four of us "Muslims" who remained.

I told the gang that I was getting the dope from a Mafioso contact I had from New York and only I could pick up the marijuana.

I would pick up the marijuana every every couple of weeks and even though I was to live in Washington, D.C. and New York—and travel to the Caribbean—I never did miss my pickup from O'Connor or Kizenski by more than a week or so, and I would fly back to San Fancisco when I made the pickup.

The "gang of five" Muslims began to get a reputation in the Bay Area as a dope subculture.

I had been in San Francisco less than a month, when one morning our "gang of five" was gathered around the television looking at the local San Francisco *Jim Dunbar Show*. And he announced that he had in the studio the charismatic Huey Newton, who was out of jail, and the indomitable Eldridge Cleaver, by phone from the country of Algeria, where he and other Black Panthers were in exile on criminal charges. The subject of whether Chief of Staff of the Black Panther Party, David Hillard, should be demoted, which Cleaver wanted, and Newton, an old friend of Hillard's, was against. Cleaver and Newton argued over this on television, and it was to lead to a bloody war in the streets in the next week between followers of Cleaver, most notably, the New York and Los Angeles chapters, which I had a large part in organizing; and followers of Newton, which was the rest of the country.

During the Cleaver-Newton war, I met, as usual, with Ron Kizenski and Robert O'Connor. I picked up marijurana from them at San Francisco's Fairmont Hotel. Kizenski and O'Connor wanted me to contact Newton. They had information that

Newton had consolidated his elements in Oakland, calling in Panther leaders from across the country, and the street war with Cleaver had convinced him to change the direction of the Black Panther Party, and focus on the Oakland operation. They had gotten that information from other FBI informants they had inside the Black Panther Party; and they also had information that the Cleaver factions were to be ineffective in stopping Newton's plans.

It was late August when I arranged through friends in the San Francisco office of the Black Panther Party to meet with their leader, Huey P. Newton, at his Oakland penthouse apartment.

O'Connor and Kizenski had gotten the information from other FBI informants inside the Panther organization that Newton, who was in jail when I was accused, did not believe I was an FBI informant. They also been told that he liked my three books, which had been recently published, and my two short plays. All of my works to that time had political themes, mostly about the Black Panthers.

Alonzo X, my renegade Muslim brother, and I went over to Huey Newton's penthouse apartment on Lake Merritt in Oakland one afternoon to meet with him, by arrangement.

At the door to Huey's penthouse apartment, which was spartan, but with expensive pieces of furniture, was a mammoth black man, who introduced himself as Big Man. He was at least six-feet nine inches and three-hundred pounds. There were two other black men, Robert and Ben, who looked to be in their late twenties, and with mean scowls on their faces, in the living room. All three men, Alonzo and I found out, were bodyguards for Huey. They all had on shoulder holsters with pistols in them, and they searched Alonzo X and me when we came into the apartment. We were unarmed.

Huey Newton, wearing a bathrobe, was looking through binoculars out the large picture window in the living room. Big Man announced it was time to be seated, still Newton continued to stare through the picture window. He explained that he could see into the Alameda County Courthouse cell in which he spent so much time in solitary confinement the last few years. Newton was wearing pajama bottoms, and was shirtless. You could see the definition in the chest and arm muscles that Newton had built up by doing pushups in his cell. His Panther comrades had told me about this, the way they would spread any information about Newton, or Bobby Seale, either for that matter.

I opened with Newton by telling him I was sorry about the troubles he was having with Cleaver, and particularly regretted the death of Sam Napier, a Newton follower who was distribution manager of the Black Panther newspaper. I had recruited Sam to join the Panthers. Napier was bound and machine gunned in an abandoned apartment in New York, and his body burned by members of the Cleaver faction.

Newton then began to carry the dialogue. "The Cleaver faction has been expelled from the Panthers. The Black Panther Party will now try to grow above ground as a political and social issues organization. The programs of the Black Panther Party will focus on such things as the free school for black children in Oakland (which was supported by money from the federal government); and other means of fighting the poverty of black people."

He went on to state that the BPP would continue to support the breakfast program, which was nationwide; the Panther newspaper; and the free health clinics, famous for their work in exposing the black disease of sickle cell anemia. He added that these programs were being threatened because of lack of money.

Newton said he had a solution. "Focus the programs, except for the newspaper, in the Oakland area with chapters around the country sending money to the elite Panthers, as well as money from the newspaper and fundraisers, to support headquarters in Oakland."

Then came the daring part of Newton's solution: "I am going to organize armed military Black Panther squads who will be trained in hand to hand combat, weaponry, bombs, and other facets of military procedure. We will ask donations from black businesses in the Bay Area to support our community programs, and there should be no problem with them. But we will also ask every dealer of marijuana, pills, cocaine, and heroin, and every pimp and prostitute in the Oakland and Berkeley areas to give us a percentage of their earnings or they can't operate here."

I was shocked and so was Alonzo. Newton was serious. "I intend to enforce this on the street, even if the Black Panther Party has to kill some dope dealers, pimps, and prostitutes, to get the message across," he continued.

Newton then extended an invitation for me to rejoin the Party as a member of the Elite Central Committee. I said that I would have to think about it, and would send my answer through one of his San Francisco emissaries.

During Newton's dramatic dialogue, one of the bodyguards passed a silver plattter with lines of powder white cocaine, and we snorted with the silver coke spoons on the platter.

When Alonzo X and I left that night, both of us agreed that we were glad San Francisco was not in Newton's plans. I suggested that we send Newton a pound of our best marijuana each week, and only communicate with him by telephone occasionally—and through his henchmen. I thought Huey was in over his head, and I stuck to our plan of not meeting with Huey Newton privately again until 1979, although most of the time I was right across the Bay and in contact with his Black Panther Party subordinates.

The reason I didn't contact him more often, or accept his offer was that in my weekly meeting with O'Connor and Kizenski they told me not to join the Party again, but help the Panthers self-destruct by trying through subtle writing to get Muslims and other black intellectuals against Huey Newton and the Black Psanther Party. The FBI agents were sure that the Party would lose the war against Oakland's dope dealers and pimps through the process of attrition by warfare in the streets.

It was while dealing dope with Alonzo X and the gang that I conceived the idea of a Pan-African community theater. I was going to name it the African Peoples' Theatre. I called Roberto, the African leader from the country of Zaire, who made the CIA deal with me in Nigeria. He thought it was a good idea, and wished me well, "and a speedy return to Africa with some black American recruits."

I felt the first step in creating the African Peoples' Theatre off the ground was to stage a cultural festival, with the backing of important people in the black American cultural movement. I wrote letters to several of the chairmen of Pan-African Studies departments in northern California.

I was contacted back by the Pan-African Studies Department at San Jose State University, and Delores Cayou at San Francisco State. I was to meet with them countless times.

I became a friend of Delores Cayou, a thirtyish black professor and dance instructor at San Francisco State University, and an ardent Pan-Africanist. I would go by her house many days to talk politics with her African friends from the continent. They were Socialist, and queried me as to why, with my background as a socialist, I seemed attracted to nations and liberation groups in Africa which were American, or CIA supported. One of my early articles, "Pan-African Socialism", had appeared in the popular journal, The Black Scholar. It was later to be reprinted in the book: *The Best of the Black Scholar: Pan-Africanism*. This article became required reading among students in Pan-African Studies, and was the guidepost by which these African intellectual friends of Delores' judged me.

I was asked by her to join the faculty at San Francisco State University—to teach Black Drama—because she was excited by my idea of a black community theater in San Francisco. I accepted the offer beginning September, 1971, with a contract extended to June, 1972.

I began to womanize again as soon as I got to San Francisco in August, 1971, and moved into Alonzo X's apartment. For a while I dated an old flame, television commentator Carolyn Cravens, who was then living in San Francisco and who, in ensuing years, was to become a popular television and radio host in the Bay Area. Then there was Janice Cobb, who was to become a medical doctor; Carrie Mae, who worked as a secretary for a black dentist friend of mine who was also a publisher; Hattie, president of the Black Student Union at California State University, Hayward, and who I was trying to get to support the Black Cultural Festival; and Penny, who worked at San Francisco State University. All these chicks were black, and this lasted from August to November, 1971, with me interchanging between the women, until I met Cynthia Watson, a fine, dark-complexioned student who was to become my steady lady.

I love women, but it was more than just that; it was also because I had lost my first wife, Robin that I was on an ego trip with women.

I reverted back to an old habit, a habit I had started in college. During my days at Golden Gate University Law School—1963-1965—I would frequent the whore stroll with my friends, usually fellow law students who were white, and we would buy black prostitutes.

They were fun. For ten dollars, and two dollars to rent the room from the prostitute's landlord, you could get an orgasm with some straight sex. For fifteen dollars, you could get a half-and-half, oral and straight sex. The price stayed the same from 1963 until the 1970s, and I was one of the best customers in San Francisco, and everywhere else I traveled.

Contrary to what some people believe, at least in those days, prostitutes were very clean, frequently visiting black doctors that I knew. I have had venereal diseases three times, and none were contacted from black prostitutes that I have taken to bed.

Years later, when I was going through psychiatric therapy, the conclusion was reached that not only was I high off alcohol every time I beat a woman, but I had picked up the habit from my environment

John Horn, Jack Willis, and myself were friends in the early 1960s in San Francisco. John Horn was a pimp, with a prostitute named Jamaica. Several times with Jack, I would be over at John Horn's and he would beat Jamaica to make her put on a lesbian show for us with another chick who we would have picked up. Then John would let us screw Jamaica, and of course the other chicks; it was called "chippying." I was still friends with Jack and John when the FBI began following me.

I had gone to bed with so many of the black prostitutes in the Fillmore area of San Francisco that I became known by name.

Then a bad thing happened. I had had sex with a black prostitute, then pulled a gun on her, and told her I wasn't paying. It was about 1967, when I was with the Black Panthers, and we controlled the streets of San Fransisco.

And the next time I had sex with a black whore in the Fillmore district, I did the same thing.

Neither time did I rob them because I had money. The word spread in Fillmore and none of the black whores would let me be a customer of their's. The reason that I would do this—pull a gun on a whore—was because the Black Panther Party, being for revolution, had little respect for pimps, prostitutes, dope dealers, and other hustlers in the black community at that time.

When I came back to San Francisco in August, 1971, there was a whole flock of new black whores who didn't know me. I began to run them, although I was, at the same time, having sex with my regular girl friends, including the freakish Carrie Mae, who loved oral sex.

I've always said until recently that I loved women with "a little dog in her." That refers to a raw woman; and the prostitutes with their mini-skirts, boots, and bold stances on the corners, got up my sexual nature.

Whenever I didn't have a date to go to dinner, drink, smoke marijuana, snort cocaine, and have sex, I would go buy a prostitute. In fact, there was a high yellow complexioned black prostitute in her twenties named Judy, who used to wear her mini-skirts up her naked behind, who I started to pimp.

I liked her because she liked me, and when I started buying her, she wouldn't play by the prostitute game; that is whenever you had an orgasm you would have to get up.

I would keep fucking Judy after I came, until I got a second orgasm. Then we would lay in the bed and talk. I know it is hard to believe, but we were like lovers.

Then Judy started refusing money for sex. One night she invited me to her home, a suburban house in San Francisco, and while snorting cocaine, she asked me to be her pimp.

I told her I would give her an answer in a few days. We had freakish sex, with her putting cocaine around my genitals, and her licking the cocaine off, and sucking.

When I got home that morning I became paranoid. Why did Judy, the star whore in the district, want me to pimp her? I was crazy about her, but I didn't come on as a pimp. Cool, of course, but not a pimp. Was the Mafia working through Judy to get at me? That's all I could figure.

So I avoided Judy, and the whore stroll. I liked the FBI image with the Muslims dealing dope better.

It was around November, 1971, and I had been off the whore stroll for about two weeks, when I met New York Broadway black producer Ashton Springer—a huge man—through Woodie King. Ashton had the Pulitzer Prize winning black play, *No Place to Be Somebody* in San Francisco.

I told Ashton about my plans to start a black cultural theater in San Francisco. And, over mounds of marijuana, which we smoked with his friends at his rustic home in the chic Sausalito area, he gave me the name of a young white chick, Michelle, who was an executive in stage and who he felt could help me get my theater off the ground.

CHAPTER XI

The Black Cultural Theater

Michelle was to be pivotal in the formation of the African Peoples' Theatre. It was November, 1971, and I was teaching drama at San Francisco State.

I had set dates of December 3 and 4, 1971, at San Jose State, San Francisco State, and the Harding Theater in San Francisco for the Black Cultural Festival. I paid the auditorium fees with my personal money, and the salary for the performers was to come from the money the two colleges gave me. I had booked two popular 1960s style black cultural acts: poet Don L. Lee from Chicago; and the dynamic Original Last Poets who were from New York.

I was to pay out of my pocket for their hotel rooms and the airfares for the four of them (the Original Last Poets was a trio). They would be paid the four-thousand dollar performance fee—a thousand dollars each—from the fees the colleges paid us; and I hoped to pay for for the local talent, as well as pay myself back for hotel, airfare and other expenses. I also hoped to make a profit.

It was a gamble, hoping to start a black community theater—and a big reason that it worked was because of this white chick named Michelle.

Contact was made by me, via telephone, after Ashton Springer, who she was working for, had contacted her first.

I arranged to meet her at her apartment.

I went there feeling optimistic about meeting Michelle. She lived in an expensive neighborhood. She was a gorgeous blond, and was wearing a mini-skirt, and sitting across from me as we started talking informally over cognac, marijuana and cocaine. I could see up her shapely legs to her drawers.

Michelle was loose, friendly, and we were soon sitting on the same sofa and French kissing. She then refused me sex, and I slapped her two or three times. I was overwhelmed by her and didn't wait to get back to the bedroom. We got up, and went to the living room wall, and I pulled her dress up, pulled her drawers down, and with as stiff as erection as I get, I went up inside her and began screwing her as we stood up against the wall.

After I got an orgasm, I got on my knees and sucked Michelle's vagina.

I was to meet her the next day, and every evening for the next week or so, as she instructed me as how to get the legal papers and budgets together for the African Peoples' Theatre.

First there was the two-set, the Articles of Incorporation, and the by-laws; which were about fifteen pages of legal matter.

I talked about my political background to Michelle; and told her that although the majority of blacks in the Bay Area supported the Black Panther Party, I felt they had gone astray from their original purpose. I told her that I had made a deal with the CIA supported African leader to recruit the politically active ones, if possible, to work in military and skilled political positions in African liberation groups.

Or at the very least, to have these politically active blacks to become fundraisers and lobbyists for Capitalist-supported liberation groups in Africa, right here in the America.

I wanted the theater to be a vehicle for this propaganda effort, and Michelle went along with this program.

Michelle also told me how to get a fictitious name document with the City of San Francisco, so that I could start a bank account under the name of the African Peoples'

Theater. One of the most important things that Michelle put together for me was the budgets for three years.

The budget for the first year, which was to be 1972-1973, because of the funding cycle, was to be for forty-five thousand dollars; and for the second year, 1973-1974, it was to increase to sixty thousand dollars; and for the third year to jump, according to our master plan, to proposals totalling 1.2 million in foundation grants.

To get funding, Michelle made contacts for me with the San Francisco Arts Commission, the San Francicso Foundation, Crown-Zellerbach Corporation, and told me to contact my friend, Woodie King.

King got me in contact with a large, black, dynamic man named Vantile Whitfield, who was to become my friend. Whitfield, who controlled a community theater component of the federally funded National Endowment for the Arts, was to match dollar for dollar the grant from the San Francisco foundations, which also included a grant from the United Presbyterian Church that I secured from my contact with Yenwith Whitney, who I had met in Tanzania.

I was not to have a problem with the Feds or the state tax agencies. Michelle and I very carefully filed with Federal and State Internal Revenue Services.

I filed taxes according to my budgets, which I followed religiously—and I was the first, and only black community theater owner to pay performers and staff. I received no money from the theater, although I invested thousands of my own money during the first year of operation in order to get it off the ground.

It was during the short time I spent with Michelle, only a week or so, that the foundation for what became the most publicized and critically acclaimed black theater in San Francicso up until that time was set up. And I have to thank her for that, for she even made the contacts with the national and local press.

That week, now that I think back on it, was too short. For not only did we have a intellectual relationship, we had a wonderful sexual relationship, as well.

She was to leave for Detroit to be on the road for a Broadway show, as an administrator. I missed her for I had fallen in love with her. I wanted her to be vice-chairman of the African Peoples' Theatre, but she was to be gone for a couple of years.

It was November, 1971, and time was getting short before the Black Cultural Festival. I flew to New York and went to a well-known restarant on 23rd Street where Shelley, my old girlfriend, was working as a barmaid.

She was glad to see me, and was happy to hear that I had done well as a writer and was starting my own theater company.

Shelley knew I liked variety in women, so she introduced me that night to a beautiful white woman named June, who was in her med-twenties and who Shelley said was a "black celebrity fucker." We drank together.

June and I left together that night and went around to my hotel, the Statler Hilton. I had some pot and cocaine.

Then June and I got naked—we were very high by this time. We started having sex by doing the sixty-nine.

June and I didn't get any sleep that night, as we tried many sexual positions, and each of us got off three or four orgasms. We, of course, rested and engaged in foreplay and oral sex between each one.

That morning we showered together and I asked June to come to London with me that night. She said she would.

I had called Roberto in Zaire (then the Congo), and told him I would meet him in London and that I needed ten-thousand dollars more to start my theater company, which was to be the vehicle by which I to get publicity for CIA-supported African liberation groups and African countries for America. Roberto had agreed to meet me in London.

That night, without any sleep for two days; June and I took the overnight flight from JFK to London. We slept on the plane.

Roberto met June and me at the airport in London. We took

his limo to the Hilton, where we had breakfast.

I gave June some money and told her she should visit the Chelsea and SoHo districts of London. June said she would return by evening.

Roberto complimented me on my taste in women. African elitists are big on white women. We then got down to the business at hand, because he had to go back to Africa that night.

Roberto told me he had seen the French edition of my book *Picking Up the Gun*. He asked me how my books were doing. I told him they were doing well—and they were—although I hadn't realized any royalties, because I was still paying back the advances. I told him of the publicity I had gotten—over two-hundred newspaper and magazine articles.

Roberto asked me if the environment in San Francisco was hostile to me, since the Panthers were very active there. I told him that I had been able to neutralize the pressures of that as well as the fact I was a suspected FBI informant.

Although the Panthers at that time had a food program for poor blacks, they had discredited themselves by killing off nearly two-hundred of their own members—mostly after accusing them of FBI activity. And since so many Panthers were being so accused, the fact that fingers were pointed at me wasn't taken too seriously in some quarters. They had also terrrorized black political and cultural activists, as well, who were not Panthers. Too, followers of Black Panther leaders Huey Newton and Eldridge Cleaver had killed each other in an internal struggle for power.

So, as I told Roberto, the Panthers had their hands full what with many black activists discrediting them, so it would appear to be that I was the least of the Panthers problems at the moment.

I also told him that I had three college speaking dates the next month, in December 1971, and that I would speak about Pan-African capitalism; and that I would inaugurate the African Peoples' Theatre that week with the Black Cultual Festival.

I was reminded of my two books on Africa I'd promised to write. I replied that I would finish them by 1972. I never did though because the political climate in Africa changed so quickly.

He gave me a certified check for ten-thousand dollars and left the dinner table to catch his plane for Zaire.

I felt confident having the money in hand. I knew then the Black Cultural Festival would be a great success because I could pay for the all the talent that I wanted.

June returned that evening, telling me how much she loved London. I told her Roberto had complimented her looks, and she returned the compliment by saying what a good looking man he was. We went out to Ronnie Scott's jazz club in SoHo for dancing that evening.

The next morning June and I flew home. I checked back into the Statler, which was full of blacks for a conference on civil rights initiated by Jesse Jackson.

I attended the job fair that Jesse Jackson had set up that afternoon. That evening I met briefly with black filmmaker and actor, Melvin Van Peebles at his Broadway play, *Ain't Supposed to Die a Natural Death*. He had expressed interest in making a film based on my book on the Panthers.

I contacted black dance professor Dolores Cayou, who had brought me to San Francisco State University to be her professional colleague.

We met that night at her apartment. It was a long night, discussing the local artistic groups, dance and music, that we would use in the Black Cultural Festival.

We came up with a list of seventeen groups, all of which were her contacts because she was very popular and experienced in the cultural scene in the Bay Area.

I committed my ten-thousand dollars to pay for the seventeen dance and music groups. Canyou was to contact the groups, each of which had many members, during the next few weeks and get a commitment from each of them to perform the three weeks of concerts at the Black Cultural Festival.

I was excited by our fruitful work night, and although she didn't partake, I was high from drinking wine and smoking dope.

I asked her to go to bed with me, because I was crazy about her. She said that she had a boyfriend. I was infuriated and beat her and forced her to have sex with me.

The next morning I was sorry, but she didn't mention what happened and we remain friends until today. She never discussed that night, but she propably knew then what was to come out in my therapy later—that I had a big problem with alcohol.

It was during this time that I was to meet a young woman who was to become my second wife. She was a nineteen year old black student who had an infant son. She was of reddish yellow complexion, and had hazel eyes—an exotic look. She was in my drama class, and what attracted me to her was her laugh and energy. She was a dancer and my best student. She was Gail Smallwood and since has changed her name to Gayle Shields.

Gayle was working as a prop mistress on my two one act plays and I wanted her to act. And even though she had a reputation in San Francisco black theater she preferred not to.

One day I invited her to a San Francisco nightclub, to see a black group, young women who called themselves French Toast. They wanted me to manage them.

After the performance I invited her to my apartment. We smoked marijuana, and talked. Early in the morning I made a move to her. She refused and headed to the door. I caught her and slapped her hard several times.

I had sex with her that night and instantly she became my girlfriend. I dropped Cynthia, Janice, Carrie Mae, Bhavanada, and Penny. Carol Cravens had long since sought greener pastures.

The Festival went off December 3 and 4, 1971. However, three days before, I went on my college tour to Indiana, Pennsylvania, and then to Louisiana to an all black college,

Grambling.

I was to speak about my experiences in the movement, and why black students needed to accept Pan-African capitalism, and look toward a return to Africa. I spoke to full houses.

I ran into black nationalist fanatics in Indiana who clashed over their versions of the various tactics needed in leading the movement. As usual I would speak, then gather with smaller groups for a question and answer period.

At all three colleges, as was true with all the colleges I ever spoke at—except when accompanied by my first wife, Robin—I became turned on to young black coeds, and I would choose one to have sex with that coming night.

I came back to the Bay Area the day of the Black Cultural Festival. It opened at San Francisco with my two one act plays. Later that afternoon, poets Don L. Lee and the Original Last Poets performed, followed by the seventeen local music and dance troops.

It was a great success, and later was to be moved to a San Francisco theater. All three performances were sellouts with the smallest crowd being two thousand.

I was very happy, because the Black Cultural Festival not only received local publicity, but national exposure through the Associated Press.

I was also in love, for Gayle Shields was not only exotic, but we seemed to be sexually attuned.

It was a good thing for after the Black Cultural Festival I had received a letter from Robin that she was having a baby by another man and wanted a divorce.

She did get a divorce on the grounds of mental and physical cruelty. She also got a police restraining order so that I could not go near her, as it was legally adjudged that I had physically abused her in the past.

I was lucky that destiny had given me a new physical and spiritual mate, or I would have been devastated by the divorce.

At this time, I was still picking up the marijuana from FBI men, O'Connor and Kizenski. I couldn't seem to get out from under their pressure on me. I was afraid that if I did, they would trump up some charge against me. The charge they always threatened me with was the conspiracy to commit murder for the 1967 Hunter's Point killings. I was also afraid that they would put out the word that I was an FBI informant. At that time, that would have been the kiss of death for me.

CHAPTER XII

Theatrical Highs, Credit Card Lows

As 1972 came in I was determined to build the African Peoples' Theatre into a viable institution in San Francisco. Gayle Shields was now secretary-treasurer of the organization.

I had run into a tall, light-complexioned young black man named Diallo, who wanted to be involved in revolutionary politics, and who would hang around my Victorian flat in San Francisco.

I was recruiting him, as well as five or six other young black men—students at San Francisco State—as organizers to further recruit others into the CIA-supported black liberation groups fighting for independence in Africa.

Diallo was strangely missing from our group for a couple of weeks, then one night he sudden appeared at my door when Gayle was over visiting. He was excited and told me that he wanted to hijack an airplane to Cuba, because he was tired of living in racist America.

I told him that black revolutionaries from America were not as welcome in Cuba as they had once been in the 1960s, because Black Panther Party members had gone there and become part of the criminal element, accused of killing Cuban nationals and killing and raping Cuban women.

Although it was not known publically, Cuba's Fidel Castro

now frowned upon black American revolutionaries. I told Diallo that I had known this since 1969 when I was in New York and had visited the Cuban mission to the United Nations for a dinner party with H. Rap Brown, James Forman, and Irving Davis. They treated us cordially enough—probably because we had had our own problems by then with the Panthers.

I told Diallo that if he did successfully hijack a plane, he would have to do hard labor in sugar fields when he got there. He said he would reconsider, but that night Diallo, obviously not having believed a word I'd told him, hijacked a plane and directed it to Cuba. The media accused him of a number of crimes, none of which I knew anything about. Obviously, he was a desperate man.

A couple of years later, while I was visiting the Cuban mission, I asked about Diallo. It took weeks before the Cubans gave me an answer. And when it finally came, it was as I expected: Diallo was working in the fields in Cuba. However, he was not treated as a political prisoner.

I kept very busy going into 1972. I stayed organized. I would start my day by going to the gym, six days a week. I started this routine in 1968, and followed it religiously in whatever city I was in. I would work out at least two hours at a time, whether it be swimmimg, lifting weights for tone, or playing basketball. And I kept this up until 1975.

I was in good physical shape, even though during this period I would still do alcohol and drugs. I also ate very well, for the first time in years. Gayle and I would eat two or three times out a week. During this period we went to many fine restaurants.

I was, however, influenced by what Gayle ate. She is a ova-lacto vegetarian; meaning that she only ate fish and fowl. Mostly I would follow the plan, but from time to time I would eat steak or prime rib but never any pork.

I was involved in the organizing committee for African Liberation Day, scheduled for May, in which black activists as well as black politicians would give speeches celebrating

Africa, and great men from Africa.

The rallies for African Liberation Day were held in San Francisco and Washington, D.C., and 1972 was to be the first of what was hoped would become an annual event. When the African Liberation Day rallies were held over 25,000 people showed up in San Francisco, and 50,000 in D.C. It was a great compliment to myself and the committee that organized the event.

I attended the conference in Washington, D.C. preceding the rally, and then flew back to the Bay to attend the other rally. I had been named chairman of the committee in San Francisco as I had a reputation among black activists because of my books and plays. I talked to the other members of the committee about organizing to send blacks from America to Africa to work, as well as to fight in African liberation struggles. It was also a favorite theme at the rallies.

I felt good that I was working within the framework of the African leader Roberto, who had given me twenty-thousand dollars earmarked by the CIA for me to organize blacks in America to go to Africa. I also did a six month stint as chairman of the FESTAC Organizing Committe. It was to be a black American cultural arts festival held in Lagos, Nigeria; and it was finally to be held in November, 1975, and although I didn't go, I was proud of the time I spent in the organization.

I was very controversial among the black American and African activists that I worked with, organizing the Pan-African political rally and cultural arts festival. They were Socialists, and they knew I was a Pan-Africanist capitalist and favored American involvement in Africa, and CIA style politics.

They favored Soviet and Chinese backed African socialist nations and leaders. We had many a heated discussion on African policy, and I was always in the minority, but I held my ground.

During this period, January to June 1972, I was in touch with the foundations to get funding for the African Peoples' Theatre. Also the newspapers in the Bay Area were doing interviews with me, and articles on my activities concerning the theater company.

By June, 1972 I had raised forty-two thousand dollars from foundations for the first season of the African Peoples' Theatre. A large share of the money came from the National Enowment for the Arts in Washington, D.C. I made several trips to the Capitol and New York to raise money for the community theater.

Also, I was working on a Broadway play about the Algerian revolutionary, Franz Fanon for Woodie King, Jr. and Motown. The project was speculative, and finally fell through. Unfortunately I never made any money off it.

My relationship with Gayle Shields was becoming more intense by now. We would spend every weekend together, going to restaurants, discos, bicycling and horseback riding, seeing movies, and going to concerts. We were constantly on the go, and I was very much in love with her.

There was only one incident to mar our beautiful relationship. For some obscure reason she had to pass up seeing me on my birthday; and when I saw her the next night I got angry and slapped her, blackening both of her eyes.

I was mostly seeing Gayle on weekends but during the week I was still having sexual encounters with the San Francisco whores, mostly Judy, who did not charge me any money. Several times I went to her expensive home in the suburban Pacifica area of San Francisco. Judy had no pimp and made good money; her ex-boyfriend was a dope dealer who had paid for the house, but was then spending time in the penitentiary. Judy now wanted me to be her new boyfriend. I wanted to stay with Gayle, though.

Judy and I finally had a big argument about Gayle, and I had to beat her, not just slap her, because she fought back. I was never to see her again.

About this time, I was not only writing the musical for Motown, I was working on a three-act drama about revolutionaries becoming dope dealers. It was based on the Panthers, who, by this time were heavy into dealing narcotics.

I called the play *A Long Way From Here*. Gayle played the female lead. It opened in June of 1972 in the Little Theatre at San Francisco State, and got glowing reviews from Bay Area newspapers. It sold out every night of the run.

I was very happy with Gayle. Not only was she a talented actress and student, she was also into health and taking care of herself. She not only would not do coke, she didn't want to be around it. I had wanted to get away from the coke influence and Gayle help me to finally quit using.

One day she called me, and told me she wanted to talk to me about something important. She told me she was pregnant. I was elated—it was to be my first child. I told her that I wanted her to have the baby and that I would marry her. She said that she wanted the baby, too, but she wanted to be independent, and didn't want marriage. She was from the beginnings of the feminist movement, and felt very strongly about having her independence. This was evidenced by her first son, Kante, whose father she didn't marry either.

Although Gayle would not agree to marry me, I felt like we were married because of the baby. So I decided we needed to get away on a honeymoon. It was the summer of 1972. From the day she told me that she was pregnant, we went through a phase of intense love. I stopped womanizing.

From this point we were to live together as common law spouses. I took twenty-thousand dollars in travelers checks and we left.

Gayle and I went to Los Angeles, where we stayed with my family. I got two major credit cards from my brother Ronald, who said the owner of the cards, Rhema Gray gave him permission to use the cards.

From there we went to San Diego where another conference on Pan-Africanism was being held. We stayed there a couple of days, participating in the conference, which was attended by several-thousand activists from across the globe.

From San Diego, we went to New York where we shopped, went sightseeing, and took in a few Broadway shows. Then I reported the twenty-thousand dollars of travelers checks as lost and got another twenty.

From New York we went to Barbados in the Caribbean. We lapped up the hot sun and the beautiful sea for a few weeks. I was in love with Gayle. This relationship made me want to stop being an informant. I wanted us to live in the Caribbean—that's why I stole the money.

After Barbados we went to Trinidad. Returning to the States via New York, I rented a car to drive to Washington, D.C. for a job interview. I hoped to become a professor at Howard University. When we arrived there I checked into a Holiday Inn very close to the red light district. Now that I think back on it, we must have called attention to ourselves there because of the expensive clothes we were wearing—suede and leathers, much like a pimp and his prostitute would dress.

Gayle used the credit card, and we went up to our room. I went out to see Vantile Whitfield and Robert Hooks, the actor, who had a major black theater company in Washington.

After being gone for a few hours, I called Gayle at the hotel.

There was no answer, and I got suspicious, because she knew no one in Washington. I decided to return to the hotel.

When I got there and went up to our room, I found it to be locked. I ran down the stairs, but was met in the lobby by a Clint Eastwood lookalike, a six-foot six, white detective, who jumped me from behind, wrestled me to the floor, and stuck a huge .357 magnum pistol in my mouth.

I was on my way to jail, and when I got to the station, there was Gayle in a room full of black detectives. They were looking through our scrapbook of pictures from the Islands and one of them said: "You might have had a good time, but now you're going to pay for it."

Gayle and I were booked, then separated. She was taken in a police car to the women's detention center, and I was put in an overnight jail lockup. The next morning we went to court and our bail was set at $50,000, individually.

The charge for Gayle was stealing a credit card; and for me, accessory to the theft. I couldn't bail us out—having stolen half of the $40,000 I had on me.

We returned to our respective jails and then were transferred to the penitentiary center, which was for both men and women. When I was checked in, the inmates found out about the forty grand I had and took it.

The first day there, in the overcrowded old delapadated building, which was ninety-nine percent black, I ran into a twenty-eight year old black named Bumblebee. He wanted to know what I was in for; and after I explained the situation, he said: "California Slim, that's what I'm going to call you; what are you a pretty boy or a pimp? And if you don't get your woman out of 1010 you won't have her anymore; they'll turn her out (make her a bisexual)."

I was to have problems with Bumblebee for the seventeen days I was there. He wanted to make a homosexual out of me. In fact, he said one time: "If you don't gain some weight, you'll be wearing a ring (the bride of some inmate) when you get down to Lorton (the state pen in Virginia)."

The men located on my floor were old-timers, the minimum age was about twenty-eight; and most of them had been there before.

It wasn't long before a rumor spread that a famous writer and Black Panther member was on the floor. I began to make friends by the first night. Pete Blackwell, a muscular black man, threatened Bumblebee to stop him from intimidating me, and another man named Carl, who suggested that I pimp "our" Gayle. Gradually I was introduced me to the other inmates.

I soon realized I was in a very touchy situation, so I began to speak about my black activist experiences, including trying to recruit soldiers for African liberation struggles, leaving out the part about being paid by the CIA for my activities.

I became very popular. It was during this time that prison revolts had caught on and were at an all-time high. The inmates sought out my teachings on black revolution.

The prisoners were in a constant state of anger, because the building we were housed in was mostly windowless, old and rotten, letting in cold air in the winter. There were rats and most of all, inmates would sometimes do a year or two of dead time—meaning it didn't count on the sentence—between the time they were arrested and it was determined if they were going to be sent up for time, let go, or what was to become of them.

These were a few of the flagrant conditions that the other inmates told me about in our conversations. They felt, they said, that since I was known to the press and television, that I could draw attention to the situation and make their demands known.

This idea spread and it seemed that within a few days, inmates were approaching me with the idea of staging a revolution and breaking out. I was caught in the middle. I had only planned to stay in the center long enough so that the judge could reduce the bail. And then I could get somebody to bail us out.

I didn't want to be in a prison revolt, but the inmates came to me. They wanted to surprise attack the guards on the late night shift, and take them hostage; and then ask for the media to come and hear their demands.

They had the program outlined when they approached me.

After getting the attention of the press, they were going to demand that seven inmates be taken in front of a judge downtown who could give them amnesty. They wanted me to be the spokesman, and the others would be picked because they were the most committed to the cause.

It was a wild plan, and I knew I was in over my head. I put in a call to a lawyer I got in contact with through my brother in California, Willard Anthony, and he posted bail for myself and Gayle.

We were out after seveteen days of jail. I learned that Gayle had some near misses also, as some of the women had tried to make her have a sexual relationship with them.

The day Gayle and I were released, the jail break went off just as the inmates had planed, and discussed with me. The guards were taken hostage and everything went according to plan, including black Congresswoman Shirley Chisholm (getting her there had been part of the plan all along) coming to the site with the media; and the six representatives of the inmates going into the judge's chambers, stripping down, and presenting their demands.

Agreements were made concerning the improvement of the conditions in the prison.

The next day, Gayle and I were on our way to New York for a few days, before flying back to San Francisco. Gayle wanted to get back to Kante, her infant son.

The charges were later dropped, and I was to never illegally use a credit card again. Also, I returned the twenty thousand dollars to American Express which they'd given me to replace those I'd reported as stolen.

I had missed my appointment with the FBI because one of the rules was never to call them. They always felt their phones were bugged by the Communists and the Mafia.

When I got out of jail, I wrote them a registered letter setting up a new meeting date in San Francisco. It had been the longest period I had gone without seeing them since I'd come back to San Francisco to live.

Chapter XIII

It Wasn't The Panthers That Finally got Me

It was autumn 1972 when Gayle and I arrived back in San Francisco. We were only to be there for three months, because, in spite of the arrest and other problems we'd had in Washington, D. C., I'd been promised a teaching position at Howard University and a one year contract as a guest lecturer. This excited me very much. For all the trouble I'd had there, I still liked D. C. very much. I also felt that it would be easier to raise money for the theater in the East than in San Francisco, as the ideal of my type of theater had not been exposed to people there so much. Too, I felt that I could be more effective at recruiting blacks for the CIA by putting some distance beteween myself and the Oakland based home of the Panthers.

For the short time we planned to be there, Gayle and I decided to stay at her mother's home in the Bay Area.

It was a happy time for me, as well as for Gayle. She was pregnant and we now had her year old son, Kante, with us. Her mother, Dr. Catherine Smallwood, a psychologist, was the perfect host—and the perfect mother-in-law. I always found her to be very charming, intelligent, and committed.

I kept high visibility, as Michelle and I had decided I would do the year before when we put together our plans for the theater group. I gave several interviews on the future plans of the African Peoples' Theatre to the San Francisco newspapers.

I was filled with bliss; my first child about to come. I never physically abused Gayle during her pregnancy, and never touched another woman sexually, although I did go to Washington, D.C. while Gayle and I were together to see Robin. I refused to fall prey to Robin then, and break my common-law marriage bliss, although it took all of my self control to resist. She had been my first wife and left me heartbroken, but now she she seem to be looking for a way to break up my relationship with Gayle.

Back in San Francisco, Gayle and I put in a lot of hours working on our theater venture again since our last production had been the past summer, and we felt it important to keep the name and idea of the African Peoples' Theater name before the public.

O'Connor and Kizenski were getting more and more interested in the theater company because of the all the exposure I was getting in Bay Area newspapers and radio.

They came up with a new plan which they ran past me, which they said it was fail proof. The plan was for me to try to escalate the friction between the Black Muslims and the Panthers, as the BPP had now moved into the drug dealing business.

The African Peoples' Theater presentation of the previous summer, about revolutionaries turning to drugs, was used as propaganda by ex-Black Panthers who were against the Huey P. Newton drug dealing faction that now claimed to be the only Panther Party. O'Connor and Kizenski obviously felt it would serve their purposes—whatever they were—to instigate another street war between the Newton faction and the former Panthers, whose symbolical leaders were Eldridge Cleaver and myself. Too, they figured that the Black Muslims might also go against the new Huey P. Newton-led Black Panther Party.

O'Connor and Kizenski, through FBI informants in all the various factions, felt my writings might trigger warfare in the streets, and as well as among members of various fractions of former BPP members who were serving time behind penitentiary bars.

We decided we would do my plays that had been done at the Black Cultural Festival, and which had been done in New York in 1970: *The Misjudgement* and *Charlie Still Can't Win No Wars on the Ground.* We ran them under the name *Babylon.* When they were done in December, 1972 at a rented theater in the Potrero Hill section of San Francisco they played to capacity audiences.

Gayle and I didn't stay in San Francisco for the entire duration of the performance run, but did stay long enough to see droves of Black Panthers and Black Muslims come to see the two plays, which had quickly become a topic of conversation among black activists in the area.

While the plays were running, Gayle and I went back to Washington, D.C. to live. Gayle was to attend Howard University as a drama student, and I was to teach European Theater, also at Howard.

It was December, 1972, when we moved into a luxury apartment complex in Washington. We had Gayle's young son Kante with us.

Both of us would come to love the Washington area, as well as the people at Howard. It was an exciting time for black culture, and one of the sources of that excitement was the Black Repertory Company, which had two directors: Vantile Whitfield, also known as Motojico in African, and the popular black actor, Robert Hooks.

They influenced the way Gayle and I thought about theater and it was Motojico who influenced me to do a production of African ritual theater, which was later performed in San Francisco during the summer of 1973, receiving rave reviews.

Gayle and I were constant companions, as well as being lovers, and in April, 1973, she gave birth to my first and only child, Maat Kamilah Anthony. I was overjoyed.

But as soon a the baby was born, I began my womanizing again. It began with a lovely, dark-complexioned black student, who a few years after was to become a highly paid model.

I had taken Gayle to the hospital the morning of April 6, 1973, when she went into labor. Mrs Jennings, a black woman who was our maid, stayed with Kante.

It was about 11 a.m. that morning when Gayle gave birth to this bubbling eight pound six ounce baby girl, Maat.

After seeing Maat, I went back to the university. Gayle and I were fancy dressers then, wearing a lot of matching suedes and leathers, even matching silk underwear.

In fact, our dress was so colorful that the word spread around campus that not only was I a teacher, but that I was also dealing dope as well.

It was at my office at school where this young black woman struck a pose at the door.

I knew who it was immediately because she was considered the most beautiful woman on campus.

I said her name and let her know that I knew who she was.

The young woman was, of course who I thought she was. She quickly congratulated me on the birth of Maat. I asked her to come help me celebrate and asked her out to dinner and drinks.

We went to a seafood place. All I could talk about was my first child. From dinner we went to my apartment, which was furnished lavishly.

There, we drank wine, smoked marijuana, and snorted cocaine.

I asked the beautiful young student to go to bed, and she immediately agreed. It was a sensational experience. I had resisted Robin while I was in D.C. on a visit a little while before we moved there—because I feared her breaking up my relationship—but now I had fallen into the trap with the lovely student.

The affair was to go on from that day in April, until I left Washington in June—and only the child, Maat, was to keep our my relationship with Gayle together.

It was only a few weeks after our daughter was born that

Gayle got the word that her sister, Cindy Smallwood, had died in a automobile accident.

It had happened late the previous night, while Cindy, who was a member of the Black Panther Party, was driving in a San Francisco rain storm. Weary from the work she had done for the Panthers—between the free breakfast for black community children, and the campaign to elect the chairman of the Panthers, Bobby Seale, the Mayor of Oakland—she'd been on the go night and day.

Gayle, Kante, the newborn Maat, and I went back to San Francisco for the funeral.

I had been coming to the Bay Area once every two weeks to deliver the large amount of marijuana I obtained through my FBI men, O'Connor and Kizenski. I had learned that I was popular among the rank and file Panthers because of my writings, and double life as a drug dealer. So I didn't fear going to Cindy's funeral, even though I knew there would be a lot of Panthers in attendance.

And as I expected, there were a lot of my old Black Panther buddies there.

There was no conflict, even from Elaine Brown, my former girlfriend and now a Panther leader.

Back in 1968, Brown had come around my to the home of my parents in Los Angeles, trying to find my whereabouts. That was when the Panthers had a contract out on my life. I thought that my play about the confrontation between a Black Muslim and a Panther would have stirred resentment among the Black Panther Party members. However, it didn't, but the FBI scam was working, because the Panthers' animosity toward the Black Muslims was stronger than ever before.

After we got back to Washington, I was to continue my womanizing. Not only was I having sex with Gayle, and the beautiful student who would become a famous model, but I started "hanging" on the whore stroll in D.C.

Most of the whores, if they didn't know me, would ask, "Are you a pimp, or the police?" They would ask me this because of my fancy clothes.

After I told them I was neither, they would say: "Show me your dick!" Evidently the police couldn't do that. I would show them my penis. Then I would pick up one of the whores.

This became a regular routine, having sex with whores and although Gayle didn't say anything, I think she knew about it, and also about my affair with the beautiful student.

I met a very talented black woman director, Glenda Dickerson, through my friend Vantile Whitfield. I signed her to direct a ritual drama that summer of 1973, and conduct workshops in drama, dance, and music.

In May, I flew to San Francisco and rented a theater in the Potrero Hill section, and also rented two penthouse apartments, one for Gayle and myself, the other for Glenda Dickerson and her husband. Then I auditioned over two-hundred blacks, who were to participate in the workshops, and from which the performers for Glenda's ritual would come.

The African Peoples' Theatre had become well known in the Bay Area, thanks to the excellent prior productions, and the resulting newpaper and radio publicity. I then flew back to Washington assured that we were going to have the best season ever.

In June, Gayle and I, with the two children, and Glenda and her husband Ronnie, with their infant daughter, flew to San Francisco. We started the workshops immediately, and after a few weeks, began rehearsals for the ritual—which was written by Glenda Dickerson, and called *The Unfinshed Song*.

Gayle was one of the best performers that Glenda had. However, they clashed because Glenda was always trying to set me up with other black women in the company.

I did continue to have affairs with other women, even with my former wife, Robin, who was now in Denver. The tension was high between Gayle and me, and a couple of times I resorted to slapping her.

I was miserable, because I loved Gayle and my new family. But I would drink, smoke dope, and snort cocaine, and I would get high and become violent toward Gayle who would try unsuccessfully to fight me back.

She quit the company a week before opening night. I thought maybe what we needed was a vacation. Maybe the love affair between us a change in order to become stronger.

Gayle and I left the children in Roanoke, with my great aunt and uncle, James and Doris Witcher, and then flew to the Caribbean, to the Bahamas, where we were to spend five or six days.

We had great fun in the Islands, gambling, horseback riding, enjoying the sun, swimming, and seeing shows.

We came back to San Francisco opening night of the ritual drama. It was to be an overwhelming success with the critics, and the audiences. It ran for four weeks.

During the run of *The Unfinished Song*, Gayle and I flew back to Washington, D.C. on business.

When we got to the Hertz counter at the Washington airport, to pick up the rental car we had a reservation for, we were met by two white FBI agents.

I was under arrest for grand theft auto. They said I had rented a car in Washington, D.C. which had not been returned and which, four months later, was found in Philadelphia, Pennsylvania.

It was entrapment by the FBI, as I was later to prove in court. However, the agents took me to jail, and on the way they commented on how cool Gayle acted—and questioned me about Black Panther Party activities. The FBI agents told me that if I would give up information about murders of Panthers by other Panthers for being FBI and police informants, they would drop the charges on me.

I refused, and was in jail two days, going in front of FBI lineups for suspicion of murder, bank fraud, and robbery. This was a time when the Black Liberation Army, a spin-off of the Black Panther Party, made up of former members of the New York Panthers, were killing police, and robbing banks. The FBI knew that I had formerly associated with members of the BLA and, as my FBI files would reveal later, felt I was still associated with them.

Gayle bailed me out of jail after two days. I met with my FBI men, O'Connor and Kizenski, a couple of days after I walked from jail. They had told me after the last time I was in jail in Washington that regular FBI agents and the police did not know about the FBI informants like me from COINTELPRO, so if I was in jail more than a week, I should write them, even though the letter would probably be read by the authorities at the jail.

Gayle and I left Washington and returned to San Francisco. She did not know of my involvement with the FBI, or about my clandestine meetings with O'Connor and Kizenski. It would be years later, in the 1980s before I would tell her.

After *The Unfinished Song* completed its run, Gayle and I called a press conference and announced our African People's Theater plans for the rest of 1973 and 1974.

That afternoon Gayle and I, and the children, left for a vacation in the Caribbean that was to last three weeks.

First, we went to the Virgin Islands. Gayle, who is very observant, noticed the disdain that the natives had for tourists of all colors. And even though we outwardly showed our love for black people, it was hard to ignore the arrogance they showed to us. I had experienced this in Africa, but Gayle said it also happened sometimes when strangers tried to be friendly with black Americans.

After the Virgin Islands, we went to Puerto Rico. The holiday helped ease some of the tension between Gayle and myself. From Puerto Rico we returned to Manhattan where we were to spend fall and winter of 1973.

We lived in a three-story brownstone apartment building, with three bedrooms, in a ritzy section of town on Central Park West. I felt we had arrived; a classy Manhattan apartment, fancy clothes, money, and a reputation in the worlds of books and theater.

I was feeling very exhuberant as Gayle and I made the Broadway and off-Broadway shows, the restaurants, and on the business side, talked to potential funders of our theater in San Francisco. The two most prominent interested parties were the United Presbyterians and the Wall Street black brokerage firm of Daniels and Bell.

The reason for going to New York, and living there a while, was to build a stronger East Coast connection for the theater.

Gayle balked every time I started biting at the rein to get out of the apartment on my own. I wanted to do some womanizing—if only with whores.

I was frustrated, and would demand over and over that she express her admiration for me, incessantly asking the question: "Am I the greatest man you have ever loved?" She would refuse refused to comment on it and arguments would ensue.

Finally one of the arguments developed into a fight, and I slapped Gayle around pretty badly.

With that, she left me and took the children to Buffalo, New York, to stay with some of her relatives.

It was just before Christmas, 1973.

I flew to Jamaica for the Christmas holidays, and on the flight to the island, I ran into a young black woman named Libra, who was in the first class section with me.

I gave her a couple of autographed copies of my book and upon landing in Jamaica, we caught a cab together. We were in Montego Bay and it was beautiful. We stopped to buy some pot, and, at her invitation, I went with her to meet her boss, black jazz musician, Miles Davis, who was staying in a villa outside of Ocho Rios.

It was to be an eventful night of conversation, as Miles and I swapped words. I had to sneak in and make love to Libra while Miles slept with another woman.

Miles saw how attentive Libra was to me the next day, and asked me to leave.

I stayed the rest of the holidays at the Hilton, and at the Playboy Club. At the airport, I ran into Alex Haley of *Roots* fame. He was with black model Beverly Johnson. I had had fun, and was fully relaxed when I returned to New York. When we got there, I invited Beverly over to my place for a drink. She agreed. And, under the guise of changing my clothes, I tried to go to bed with her. This scene of stripping down to my shorts, offended Beverly very much. I never really got over being embarassed about that.

Back in New York, the stock brokerage firm of Daniels and Bell contacted me, and I went in to see them for a series of conferences. They liked my theater operation and their offer to me was fantastic. They were buying a four-story restaurant and disco on Broadway called Alexander the Great's. They wanted me to bring my shows from San Francisco to New York, and be the executive producer for a large dinner theater in Alexander the Great's. We also talked about them financing me for independent movies.

I went back to San Francisco to regroup the theater company. I now had a game plan. I checked into a motel on Lombard Street because I thought I would only be in the Bay Area for a couple of months before going back to the East Coast.

I began to scout for a dowtown San Francisco theater. I also started hanging out in San Francisco's "sin" district on North Beach, home of massage parlors and nude shows.

I had three white woman, who I was having sex with for free. They were nude dancers. We would have freak sex—although I never did group sex.

Then I met her, the white woman who I was almost to marry before I had my nervous breakdown later that year, 1974.

She was the madam at a North Beach massage parlor. A young woman of Danish descent, who was five-feet ten inches tall and had the most beautiful body I had ever seen. Her name was Christina, and she was a stunner.

I went into the massage parlor one night, with my fancy clothes, and we went to a private room and stripped naked.

Christina asked me: "Are you a pimp?"

"No," I replied

Then she asked: "Then, why is a goodlooking man like you in a place like this; you should have enough girlfriends."

I told her that I wanted to get to know her. After we'd talked for an hour or two, she gave me her address and telephone number.

We started a whirlwind love affair. I went to the massage parlor every night for six months. That is, until Gayle came back to San Francisco.

Christina would be very unprofessional, for a madam, and sometimes I would French kiss her, and fondle her privates, right in the front section of the parlor, where people from the street could see everything.

After Christina would get off at 2 a.m. we would go to breakfast and then to her apartment, where we would snort cocaine far into the morning, and then we would have freak sex. I always felt I had to suck off a white woman.

I was still meeting with O'Connor and Kizenski. They showed duplicity about my personal life. They said they were sorry that my family was broken up, but it was inevitable because they felt I was destined for the fast track with women; and that I was on the fast track with the Mafioso in North Beach.

The callousness of the FBI, and my disgust with my past activities, led me to again consider taking Gayle, the children, Kante and Maat, and going into a self-imposed exile in Dar es Salaam, Tanzania, Africa.

I wrote several letters to friends in Tanzania, and they would call me to talk about my relocating to Africa. I knew my phone was bugged and told my friends in Africa that it was. But in their enthusiasm they would call and talk freely anyway.

I believe that the FBI and CIA used my attempt to exile myself to Africa as the excuse for later using a hallucinogenic drug on me. The CIA, which operates internationally, wanted me to continue to build a base among black activists in America, I was told though my contact from Zaire, Roberto.

However, I had regouped the theater company, and we were scheduled to start rehearsals in September, 1974, to do a play I called *Time* which I had written about Gayle and my experience in the D.C. jail. I had a leased a popular theater downtown and among my actors was a well-built young black man, now a popular Hollywood actor, Danny Glover.

Gayle and the kids came back to San Francisco, so I moved out of the motel into a penthouse apartment in an exclusive building.

I went to see Christina to tell her I would be with Gayle and the kids for a few weeks. We got into an argument, and I slapped her. I would never see her again.

Meanwhile, in August, some business came up in regard to Alexander the Great's and I had to fly to New York. I took Gayle and the children with me.

On the plane I started talking to Gayle about my other women. We began to argue. I slapped Gayle, and to my surprise, she slapped me back. We continued to argue and fight all the way cross the country.

When we landed at JFK, I slapped Gayle so many times that I knocked her to the ground, then I kicked her in the side.

Gayle got to her feet and hit me with Maat's baby carriage.

I took Maat in my arms and began to leave the terminal. That was when at least a dozen uniformed police surrounded me with their guns drawn.

They told me to put Maat down and to put my hands against the wall.

I did as they ordered, all the while shouting, "Do you know who I am? I'm Earl Anthony! I'm gonna take New York!" I know they would have killed me if I hadn't had Maat. They had that killer look in their eyes.

When Gayle and Kante got to where the police held me and Maat, she shouted: "Nigga, they should cut your dick off!"

The police took Gayle, the children, and me to the station in the airport but none of us were booked.

We returned to my apartment in New York. The next day, Gayle ran back to San Francisco to stay with her mother.

That evening, after being out all day on business with financiers for my projects, I found a package in my mail box. It was some sex stamina pills that I had ordered from the September, 1974 issue of *Penthouse* magazine, the last time I was in the New York apartment.

The pills had come from Los Angeles. I wanted them because I had promised Christina in San Francisco that I would start sex orgying with her and her friends.

I took several of the sex stamina pills because I was going woman hunting that night.

It was LSD. I started tripping. I had had LSD before but never any as powerful as this.

I had to get outside. I walked the streets of New York all night, only stopping to rest in Central Park.

The next morning I flew to Los Angeles. My mother and father, Geraldine and James Anthony, picked me up at the airport, taking me straight to the mental ward of UCLA.

There, they interviewed me, and I told them that the FBI had switched LSD for the sex stamina pills at the mailbox. This was to silence me for my political background.

The doctors at UCLA admitted me and gave me a shot of thorazine—a heavy psychotropic medication.

Over the next three weeks, they were to keep me heavily sedated and I was, during therapy, telling the psychiatrists about why I felt government agencies were trying to drug me. I was seeing mostly a Dr. Regina Palley.

CHAPTER XIV

Going Crazy In LA

August and September 1974, I spent at the University of California, Los Angles Medical Center's psychiatric ward. I was being heavily medicated with the drug thorazine, and going through daily therapy sessions. My chief psychiatrist was a young female doctor, Regina Pally. I told her everthing that I could recall that had happened in my life from 1963, up to the day I had taken the LSD, which I was and still am convinced the FBI, or some other federal agency, had sent to me on purpose.

It was the first time I was in a mental hospital as a patient. The general consensus of the psychiatric team was that I had suffered a personality breakdown triggered by drugs. They tested for the acid, and found it in my system.

Between therapeutic sessions with doctors, I was allowed to participate in games like volleyball, bowling, swimming, and cards. Still medicated, I hallucinated that the FBI and CIA were coming to get me.

My paranoia reached the level where I considered it crucial to close the African Peoples' Theater. I returned all the grant money, unspent, to the respective foundations, and contacted the San Francisco Bay area news agencies to see that it was properly covered, and ask them to see it was a reported that the money had been returned.

The doctors at UCLA were not convinced that federal agencies had drugged me. Although the acid was found in my body, they thought I had taken it myself, and on purpose.

I told the doctors that they could mail order the sex stamina pills from *Penhouse* and have them tested to see if it was LSD. I don't believe they ever did this, although I showed them the advertisement. I think they thought I was tripping, and had gotten hold of some more LSD.

I was able to leave the hospital in October of 1974, and I was so happy to be released that I didn't wait for a ride home. Because I didn't have any money I walked from the UCLA hospital to my sister's house in Palos Verdes on the south bay coast of Los Angeles, a distance of about thirty miles.

I was to stay with my family, on sort of a revolving basis, first with my sister and brother-in-law, Dr. Barbara Rhodes and her husband, Russell; then with my mother and father, and with my one brother and sister-in-law, Ronald and Renee Anthony interchangeable from October to December, 1974. I was still taking thorazine, and sleeping for sixteen hours a day. I was disoriented. My family has always been close and loving, and they were very supportive, as was Gayle, and her mother, Dr. Catherine Smallwood.

I would call San Francisco a couple of times a week to see how Gayle was doing, and how our two young children were doing.

They had been shocked by the turn of events, and didn't know whether to believe my story about the drugs or if I was just crazy. At that time, although there had been rumors, neither my family nor Gayle or her mother knew definitely that I had involvement in COINTELPRO, nor about the Nigerian connection with the CIA.

I decided that I would try to write and produce film and television in Hollywood, but first I had to return to San Francisco to write some projects and see my family. I went back to San Francisco in December, 1974.

Gayle and I got a large, rundown flat in the Fillmore area. She had to take employment as a temporary clerical worker so that we could live.

Gayle, being very understanding about my breakdown, said she would always be there for me. She expressed confidence in my recovery and asked me to marry her.

We went to Las Vegas that week and were married.

Back in San Francisco I started writing film scripts. I would spend early mornings writing and then during the day, I would hang out either at the neighborhood bars with friends, or North Beach, the so-called "sin" section of the city. I was drinking liquor, benefit of my friends who were encouraging my plans for a Hollywood career.

Even though we had married, the tension between Gayle and I continued. She wanted me to get a regular job, which, as I look back on it now, I foolishly refused to do. I wanted my time to pursue my artistic endeavors. She was also unhappy over my return to alcohol, and was still bitter about my prior escapades with other women.

I tried advertising and met a large white man called Big John who worked for one of the top national advertising firms. He felt I had the touch for advertising and introduced me to Bob Dalva, who headed famed Francis Ford Coppola's San Francisco based Zoetrope Studios.

Dalva became a friend of mine, and I wrote a sickle cell anemia commercial, which was rejected by Zoetrope. But Coppola's outfit was still interested in my doing commercials. I wanted to do black film scripts but was told that black films were not the genre in which they wanted to work.

I was still into what my wife Gayle called "substance abuse" and was not taking the medication the doctors at UCLA had prescribed for me. I was also drinking heavily. Gayle got fed up and left me because I would become hostile and violent toward her after drinking.

Much of the time I has hanging out with Arthur, Keith and John Gutierrez, who were club and theater owners in San Francisco. They wanted me to go back into public funded theater. However, I was paranoid, feeling that my that the cultural and revolutionary themes of my plays would bring back attention from federal agencies. I was later to find out that the FBI did have records of my previous works including copies of the newspaper reviews my plays had received.

Before she left me, Gayle was constantly looking for jobs. Although she had attended both San Francisco State and Howard, she was now going to trade high school to pick up computer skills.

She was called to come back and have a second interview with TWA for a job as a stewardess. But the night before she was to have the second interview, I got drunk, blacked out and beat her so badly that she had to wear sunglasses to the TWA offices. She didn't get the job.

I was seeing a young, white male psychiatrist who prescribed me thorazine. I didn't take it because it made me sleep all the time.

I continued to work out at the YMCA. I was not working out six days a week as I had done previously, but more like three times per week.

I came back to Los Angeles with Gayle and Maat and Kante in June, 1975. I was scheduled to take a teaching assignment as a professor of drama at California State Univeristy at Northridge, to replace a resident professor who was on leave for a year.

Gayle and I and the children moved into a spacious well-kept apartment in the black community of Los Angeles. It was the area known as the "jungle."

Gayle looked for a job; being an independent feminist was important to her and she wanted to find a job that would offer her a career..

In September, 1975, I started teaching drama at California State University, Northridge. Gayle had landed a job at an industrial packaging plant in Hollywood. I had written several film scripts while in San Francisco. In the process of finding someone to type them, a white woman named Mia, I also met her boyfriend, Neal. He was a drug dealer, and since I was working again, I was to become one of his best customers.

I would buy two ounces of marijuana a week, costing one hundred and twenty dollars then. And when I wasn't working I would constantly be puffing on a joint. Neal had some good smoke.

We became friends. And, since he was an actor and liked my scripts, we would spend hours talking and smoking dope with his Anglo friends. From time to time, we'd snort coke.

I began to pray a lot beginning in 1974—for forgiveness from God, for all the mistakes I had made, and that my stepson, Kante, and daughter, Maat, would not be scarred by the arguing and fighting that Gayle and I did.

However, Gayle and I continued to argue, mostly because I was drinking too much, and using too much marijuana. It got so bad that our upstairs neighbor, a twenty-eight year old black ex-Army paratrooper named David, who was over six feet tall and weighed over two-hundred pounds, began to gossip about our arguments. The arguments upset me, and I spent a lot of sleepless nights. Too, the fact that David talked about us infuriated me. During these sleepless nights I would drink up to three six-packs of ale.

One night I went up to David's apartment, where he and three other black men were playing dominoes. I asked him: "Why are you gossiping about Gayle and me?"

He denied it. I called him a liar and invited him outside.

When we got downstairs, I threw the first punch, and in the fistfight that ensued, he knocked me out and was going to stomp me until Gayle ran between us. At the hospital that night they gave me halydol, to make me rest. After that I began taking the drug, but continued to drink ale, smoke marijuana, and, when I could get it, use cocaine. I was to learn the hard way that mixing halydol with anything is not a good idea.

As spring of 1976 came in, I was still teaching. My substance abuse did not affect my performance at the workplace. I was doing well there.

It was during that time, though, that Gayle and I got into an argument over my problem, but I didn't slap her. I wrestled her to the floor and began to karate chop her in the ribs.

She left that night with the kids to stay with my brother Ronald and his wife Renee for a few days.

I was miserable when Gayle left and started drinking even more heavily. I got so drunk one night that I put my fist through our large plate glass window. I cut my hand but then got to yelling, threatening my neighbors with violence. I was particularly angry with David and yelled for a rematch. The police came, because my neighbors said I had a gun. And, although I didn't, the police, seeing the window and hearing my threats, forced their way into my apartment and locked me into a straight jacket.

The police took me to the psycho ward at Los Angeles County/University of Calfornia hospital.

This was not the plush hotel-like surroundings of UCLA. No way. I woke up the first morning from the thorazine that they had injected me with the night before only to see some white dude sitting next to me jacking off.

I was to find in the three days I was at County/USC that all kinds nuts were in there with me. I was to befriend a handsome black brother named Ricco, who was in for fighting the police. From the looks of him they had beaten him badly.

Ricco's anger at society raged, and being only in his early twenties, I thought that this was a prime example of what was happening to black youth in America. I was to see him years later in jail and he was headed for the penitentiary. I was in for traffic tickets that had gone to warrant. Later he became a Hollywood pimp of white women, and was known for the black patch he wore over his left eye. He lost the eye in a fight while in prison.

He was classic in that he was caught in the lifestyle of the underbelly of society, a lifestyle which seems even more prevalent in 1989, than it did ten years ago.

While in the County/USC police ward, the doctors tried to ship me to a facility at Norwalk, California, for a long stay, but my sister said she would take custody of me. My brother came to pick me up and told me that Gayle had returned to stay with me.

I went home to Gayle and the children and finished out my year at Cal State, Northridge. Gayle was still working at the Hollywood industrial plant, and I got a job doing telephone surveys parttime. We were still living in the "jungle" and living very ordinary lives. After where we'd been, and having tasted fame and respect in the book and theater worlds, it was depressing.

By the end of 1977, I felt as if the world was closing in on me.

Nevertheless, I started lecturing at California State University at Los Angeles in 1978, teaching Afro-American History and Caribbean Literature. I was to teach there one year on a guest lecturing contract.

I was still trying to break into Hollywood. Although I did get some good responses on my scripts, I couldn't raise the capital to have anything produced.

I became so disheartened by my script rejections that I began to drink and become abusive again. Finally, Gayle and I separated. Soon afterwards she return to the Bay Area to finish her degree in Communications. She divorced me in 1980 and had a restraining order placed on me.

When Gayle left I was forced to leave the apartment, which was in her name. I moved to a motel in Hollywood. One night after I'd beeen drinking, I called a taxi to take me home from a bar. As I wasn't working and had no money to pay the cab driver, I tried to jump out when he stopped at a redlight about a block away from the motel. Well, I got into a fistfight with the driver because I jumped out without paying. Once I got away from him and was outside the cab, he chased me up onto the sidewalk tried to run me down. This was on Sunset Boulevard at night. Anyway, he crashed his cab into a building and wrecked it. We got into a fight and he blacked both my eyes. The police came and told me they would arrest me if they saw me on the streets of Hollywood again.

I checked into UCLA again, having no place to live. I was to be there for a month, undergoing psychiatric treatment.

It was there that I met a friend who was a homosexual. He was a rich hairdresser. He wanted to have an affair with me, but it never happened. However, on his passes in and out of UCLA, he would bring me drugs.

My mother and sister checked me out of UCLA and rented me a modern, apartment in the black community. I managed to pull myself together and was able to get some assignments from *Players*, a black version of *Playboy*; also *Adam*, which had once been a very literary magazine and had published some of the most famous writers of the 1960s and 70s but had become a swingers magazine.

I began to write for these publications in 1979; and I was to freelance consistently for *Players* until an incident in 1983 caused them to stop giving me assignments, but continued writing for *Adam* for another year or so. It was the beginning of my comback as a writer.

My forte was the interview. I interviewed my friends from the New York stage and film game: Woodie King, Robert Hooks, Dick Anthony Williams, Rosalind Cash, and Vonetta MGee; as well as Pam Grier, Jayne Kennedy, Eldridge Cleaver, Jamaa Fanaka, and many other stars among the black entertainment and political world.

In late 1981 I interviewed Eldridge Cleaver for *Players*. Some of the interview was a bit too hot, politically, for that publication. By that time Eldridge was a different man than the one I had known back in the Panther days in the Bay Area. He was no longer preaching a "new order" nor talking about overthrowing the government. On the contrary, he had come to the view that blacks were much better off working within the system to make changes rather than fighting it. In a way he become subdued. He had been giving some serious thought to religious matters, as you will see when you read the interview that makes up the next chapter, and was thinking seriously about becoming a Morman at one point and labeled himself a "born again Christian" at another point.

The leadership of the Black Panther Party was always very charismatic. Except for Eldrige Cleaver, who was surpisingly outgoing and more of a public person than the others, there was a mystery about the early leaders of the party. Of course, Eldridge had already published Soul On Ice *and created an image of himself in the public mind. Bobby Seale (overleaf 1) was, in those days, somewhat quiet spoken and while people got the idea that he was secondary to Huey Newton, it simply was not true as far as those of us in the party were concerned. Seale commanded a lot of respect. The overleaf photograph was taken in the early 1970s when he was running for the office of mayor of Oakland.*

Elaine Brown (overleaf 2) is shown in a photograph taken in September, 1977. Brown was the most powerful woman ever in the Black Panther Party. I found her to be an intelligent, intense woman with charm and warmth. Huey Newton (overleaf 3, in court on May 28, 1981) died an enigma. He was idolized by a generation of blacks, Latinos, and radical whites from the 1960s. But on another level in the 1970s and 1980s Newton was to make both friends and enemies because of his personal, political, and business dealings in Oakland.

The photograph of me (overleaf 4) was taken in Los Angeles in 1981 after I had recovered from my second nervous breakdown and was working as a journalist and working at converting Picking Up The Gun *into a television docudrama. The photograph was made by writer and historian Ray Locke who I met when he was assigned to help me on the television adaption of the book. He also took the photograph of Eldridge Cleaver (overleaf 5) in Los Angeles the same year when I did the interview which is reprinted in the next chapter. All photographs reprinted by permission of the Oakland Tribune unless otherwise credited.*

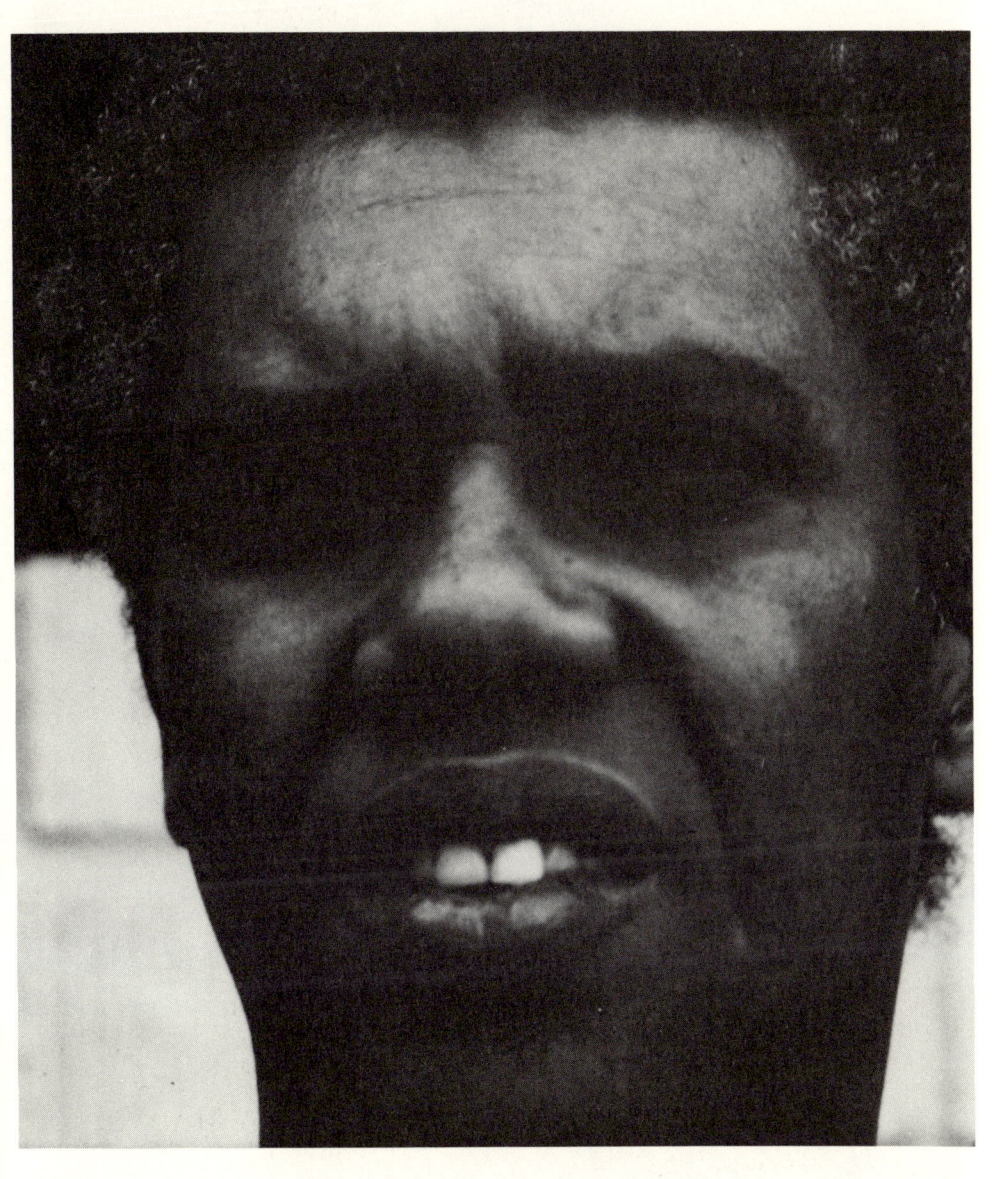

CHAPTER XV

Eldridge Cleaver Interview

Eldridge Cleaver came out of prison in 1966, after nine years of incarceration; he immediately formed the Black House in San Francisco, a black cultural clearing house in the area. He joined forces that year with Huey Peter Newton and Bobby George Seale, the co-founders of the then Black Panther Party for Self-Defense in Oakland, California. It was in this year that his semi-autobiographical cultural tome *Soul on Ice* was published and subsequently became a best seller. It was also in 1966 that Huey Peter Newton was wounded in a shootout in the Oakland streets where one policeman was killed and another wounded. Cleaver came forth to take leadership of the Black Panther Party after Bobby George Seale was incarcerated and organized the Free Huey Newton Movement. It became a national and international movement that eventually freed Newton in 1970, after he had become a national and international persona and the Black Panther Party became the revolutionalry organization of the sixties; a fact due primarily to Cleaver's leadership.

April 6, 1968, two days after Martin Luther King's death, Eldridge Cleaver was involved in a shootout in Oakland with the police, where Little Bobby Hutton, a fellow Black Panther Party member was killed, the first of many Panthers to die in the struggle for their vision of a Socialist technological state in America. Cleaver was imprisoned, released and instead of returning to prison for attempted murder, went into exile, through Montreal, Canada; escaped in disguise out of the country with the San Francisco Mime Company and went by boat into exile in Havana, Cuba. It was 1968, the year before J. Edgar Hoover, Chief of the FBI and Richard Nixon declared the Black Panther Party the most dangerous threat to America's security; the media generally concedes that Cleaver fashioned the Party's image and was chiefly responsible for building it from an Oakland organization into a widely respected national and international revolutionary force (in the interview Cleaver mentions his Cuban experiences).

From Cuba, Cleaver went to Algiers, Algeria, where he joined with his wife and fellow revolutionary figure Kathleen Cleaver and they, with other Black Panther members, formed the International Chapter of the Black Panther Party. It was 1969; and the odyssey ended in Paris, France, in 1973, with stops in Communist China, North Korea, North Vietnam, Congo Brazzaville, and Libya, spreading the Socialist revolutionary gospel in America. In 1974, he and his wife returned to the United States in the custody of the FBI (which the Black Panther Party declared in its newspaper was an FBI deal made by Cleaver; Cleaver refutes the allegation). He was incarcerated for nearly a year; then explored the ideas of the Moonies and then the Mormons, searching for religious direction. He is now (in 1981) involved as the prime mover in a petition to remove the black mayor of Oakland, Lionel Wilson. He intends also to throw his hat into the mayorial race in Oakland.

I had the pleasure of interviewing Mr. Cleaver in the *Players* magazine offices in Los Angeles. Ray Locke, who had been working with me in developing a televison mini-series from *Picking Up The Gun* for producer Ken Belsky sat in on the interview and, as he had his camera with him, took some photos of Eldridge that were later published both here and in Europe.

Anthony: Eldridge, you have been involved in controversy for most of your adult life—social, political and now religious. Do you foresee that your granting an interview to a men's magazine will cause you any difficulty?

Cleaver: I think immediately there will be a question as to why I consented to be interviewed by *Players* magazine, which I think can fairly be placed in the same category with *Penthouse, Hustler, Playboy,* or any of the others that have been controversial. And I say controversial because in recent times, Jerry Falwell filed suit against *Penthouse* for running an interview that he gave; Jimmy Carter was severly criticized for giving an interview to *Playboy* magazine, and many people were saying to me, do not give an interview to *Players* magazine because it can't help you. It will only hurt you and they will probably doublecross you and print it in such a way that it would be a very negative result. And so, first of all I told them that I felt that I could rely upon your word. that I believe that your word has some integrity behind it and that I believe that you would treat it in a fair manner and not deliverately deform or twist up my words the way some people have done.

But, most of all I believe in the example of Jesus Christ who thought that it was proper and correct for him to go amongst the sinners and not just to hang out with the people that are already saved. And he said he came to bring the sinners to repentance and not the righteous. And so, there's always been this conflict.

Anthony: Some of your more sanctimonious brethren might consider *Players* dangerous and off-limits. Why don't you share this view?

Cleaver: I think that if this kind of magazine and its readership is identified as being one of the out of bound places not to go, I think that it's keeping in character for me to rush in where angels fear to tread. Because I believe that this magazine will be read by American people. So I think it's a privlege to have the opportunity to speak to Americans within the confines of pages in *Players* magazine.

Anthony: You're not going to preach to us are you?

Cleaver: I don't have any preaching message for *Players* just to get the naked girl out of the middle. And so, I will not look hypocritically down upon other people who evidently feel that need.

Anthony: Some so-called Christians try to bury their heads in the sand and ignore or repress sexuality. They try to master sexuality by censoring it out of their own lives and out of the lives of others. Why have you, a Christian, chosen a different route?

Cleaver: I'm very interested in the pathology of sexuality in America, because I believe that we are sexually sick. However, I don't believe that repression is going to help us heal ourselves. Repression is part of the cause of this sickness, a repression so profound that it goes back to the very beginning of time and the imposition of the fig leaf upon the male form. And since that time priests and holy men have been playing around with the fig leaf and adjusting its length and finding out how much flesh could be exposed and we have gotten lost away from the very meaning of the whole thing. We don't know anymore what our true sexuality should be. We have men running around thinking that they are women men. We have confusion on our hands. The truth is, that we are lost. We don't know who we are.

Anthony: How are we to discover our most genuine selves?

Cleaver: The only guidelines that we have are those that have been handed down traditionally through the vehicle of religion where man's purpose and his destiny and his relationship with the Creator of this universe and his Creator is dealt with.

We have a situation where science came along in the last century and swept religion aside. Science was able to do this because science was dealing with concrete facts that it could weigh, measure and could be seen, touched and smelled. Whereas, religion was dealing with abstractions that couldn't even be proven and they were couched in what seemed like fairy tales and mythological formulations and we had this sad situation where the Pope of Rome, who is the most powerful and renowned religious figure in the world, seemed always to come up on the wrong side of the truth in arguments where there was nothing in the Bible that said the earth was flat, yet we had the Pope in the Vatican defending to the death, to the death of those who advocated to the contrary that the earth was flat. Great thinkers have been butchered and suppressed by religious authorities and so religion has gotten a hateful name, an evil name, and a bad reputation that has persisted over hundreds of years and it was bad in its own right but it also helped to prop up rotten and exploitative forms of government that go back deep into the mire of human past.

Now we have it coming down to us today, the very remnants of what religion should be. The grand magnificent place that religion once had in the lives of human beings has been lost and it was supplanted by the new servants on the scene, by the scientists, the Nobel laureates. The prestigious men through making their discoveries were able to masquerade as creators and that by discovering something they invented it and they became demi-gods that we worshipped for fifty years. We're at the end of that process and we are through worshipping science and we are going back to God and to the principles of our roots that are contained in our religion. This is something that needs to be brought to everybody. Not just those who never look at the magazines that contain the naked women, but also for those who read the naked women magazines, and I say I'm happy to be able to talk to these people today about these subjects.

Anthony: Do you intend to organize a religious mass movement?

Cleaver: I intend to participate in a mass movement of the American people that will be both spiritual and political. I am saying that we need a spiritual and political revival in America and I think we see the first throes of that movement coming into being.

Anthony: What causes you to believe this?

Cleaver: Because you have a situation now where people in the community are worried and afraid even about food, where their next meal is coming from and how long the food is going to last.

Anthony: And...

Cleaver: I'm concerned. I have been traveling around and meeting a lot of different people and one group of people that I have been spending a lot of time with recently are the members of the Church of Jeasus Christ of Latter Day Saints. Among many things about this church that I find very impressive is that they have a food storage program where they require all families who are members of the church to store food. These people have in their houses enough food to last them for a year or two years. They have water and all kinds of staple items stored up for one year and two years, you hear me! And you go into the black community and the people don't have enough food to last until Monday... If this is Saturday, if there wasn't no food brought into Safeway it wouldn't be no food in the community.

Anthony: The Moral Majority would have us believe our entire salvation is bound up with them. Are they the answer?

Cleaver: A lot of people do not understand what is going on with the Moral Majority.

I truly believe that if more people understood exactly what was involved, then we would have no need for a moral majority because it would be that the American people themselves would be the moral majority. We're in a situation where Jerry Falwell in American terms could amass the same kind of power that an Ayatollah Khomeni amassed in Iran, and I believe that this would be inimical to the best interest of democracy. We don't need this kind of a powerful, special interest group that is able to bludgeon other people into conformity with this particular set of views.

Now, the answer is not to fly in the face of the Moral Majority or to castigate Jerry Falwell. It's first of all to come to terms with the message of the moral majority. To evaluate whether they really have an axe to grind when they talk about the dirty TV and the sponsors and all this about the dirty magazines and the naked girls. Okay, I think that when the chips are really down on the table, if more people would be concerned about the issues and values that the Moral Majority is concerned about then we would be able to eliminate the development of this awesome energy that is now in motion and to stop it from taking an intolerant form that could be devastating towards those with whom it does not agree. We are faced with this danger and this possibility.

I, for one happen to know Jerry Falwell. I have spoken in his church to his congregation and I respect the man and I know that he is a good man. And so, I feel that it is possible to keep communication open; communication should be kept open and we should not square off against each other in any kind of fight to the death. Because in the final analysis, if people want to look at dirty books, I think in America and in the American traditions of the protection of the American Constitution, people have the right to do that.

I believe there is another problem when it comes to the air

waves and television, which is so difficult to control, and it's embarrassing to a family that is sitting there in that kind of situation and suddenly right in the middle of you here's some kind of public display of depravity. Well, I think there's a line there that needs to be drawn.

Anthony: You have been a very visible and vocal political figure in the past, Eldridge. What are your political aspirations now?

Cleaver: I think if you are talking about running for office then the only thing you're referring to is my activity in Oakland, California, running for mayor. However, I think that politics has a much broader meaning than a specific thing like that. I am interested in a political revival in America. I want to see the American people rise up in the spirit of the 4th of July and seize their destiny and this can only be done if we become very nationalistic.

Anthony: Nationalism, patriotism, those used to be dirty words to us, the people in the movement. Why should we embrace them as positive values now?

Cleaver: Because we have abandoned the American Constitution; we have strayed away from the principles that were laid down by the Founding Fathers and we have been tempted into this by unremittently following a goal of exploitation and getting rich quick—getting something for nothing. Getting involved in exploiting the world, getting involved in exploiting each other; exploiting ourselves over a long period of time including the whole experience of slavery and it has brought us to the point today where our whole society, whether you're talking about it economically, politically, morally, socially, spiritually, is in the pits of a decline.

What is commonly referred to as patriotism is really a positive orientation to the institution of your society. I believe that America is falling apart at the seams because we have a cultured people that is completely confused and divided. We have some people who are Americans and then we have some other people who are just citizens and not really Americans. They don't partake of the American Dream. They don't believe or even manifest any awareness of what makes our democratic form of government different from other forms of government. They don't understand and appreciate the great battles and triumphs and victories that were involved in creating this country. And so, I think that what we have on our hands is an ignorant, morally corrupt and misguided people who are given over to sensuality and lust and drugs and other feel-good ways of doing things including alcohol and perverted sex.

It once was a phenomenon of the urban centers of America, this corruption of the cities, but it has now spread through every nook and cranny of the land until we have truly become the very image of Babylon. now that's on the down side. On the up side we are still the most free and the most democratic country in the world. I think America is the greatest country in the world. I really feel in my heart that America really needs to take control of the world.

Anthony: Why?

Cleaver: We are faced with a hostile situation on the internatnial scene where a very powerful totalitarian force, which has consolidated rule over the majority of mankind has conquered great land masses and is now knocking at our very door in El Salvador and Nicaragua. We now have three bases of Soviet imperialism in the Western Hemishere—in Cuba, El Salvador and Nicaragua, and the American people are not clear on what their response should be to this situation.

We don't have a consensus among American people. The old consensus has broken down because of revolution and war on an internaional level. The old image of America has fallen by the wayside and we have a new America in search of balance and I really believe that it was for this day and time that God came to France and tapped me on my shoulder and said, "Eldridge, follow me." This is some six years ago and I have watched unfolding over this period a marvelous drama of America awakening and trying to come to grips with this awesome situation and I have watched the American people begin to confront each other in spirit of getting its house in order.

Now, in terms getting this house in order I am in favor of using a very strong broom because we have lawlessness from the top of this society to the bottom.

Anthony: Eldridge, what about your petition to recall Oakland Mayor, Judge Lionel Wilson?

Cleaver: Well, Mayor Wilson was recently reelected to a second term of office in Oakland and with a very token opposition and for me this was the last straw, because I know who Lionel Wilson is and what he represents and a lot of people seem to have forgotten.

Anthony: Forgotten what?

Cleaver: Wilson built a coalition that was based upon the community organizations that had been fighting the old power structure throughout history. Included in this coalition were the remenants of the Black Panther Party in the hands of Elaine Brown. And this coalition was successful in putting Lionel Wilson in office.

Well, Lionel Wilson is in office because of the black struggle and the black struggle by its definition, has done nothing but rock the boat and had that not been he would not be sitting in the pilot seat in the boat right now. And yet, here we have this man sitting in the pilot seat in the boat. And so I want to give it a try (at replacing Wilson) and so we are starting a campaign to recall Lionel Wilson. We're into his back and we're going to get him and I'm going to be the next Mayor of Oakland.

Anthony: Eldridge, you said in a speech once that in North Korea, they chop off your hands for stealing something, and therefore America's democracy is the reason that you support America. Is that the reason you support America?

Cleaver: That certainly is not, boiling it down into a nutshell, as to why I support America. I do not recall saying that about North Korea because in North Korea they blow your head off.

I am an American. I'm not just an American citizen. I partake of the Aemrican Dream. I partake and drink deeply of the American spirit. I believe that I am sort of a new Negro. I think you have to really go back historically, when we start talking about first we have the black slave, then we got the freed man. Then in the twenties we got the New Negro—we got the Negro first, then we got the New Negro. Then we got the black man, so I think we need a new black man, because this Negro we got now ain't ready yet.

Anthony: What is our flaw?

Cleaver: We look towards Africa and we don't participate fully in America. We are unattached in America, looking out of America towards Africa, but not going back to Africa has given us a form of paralysis, which I call a fence straddling mentality.

I am a black man that has gotten off the fence. I am not looking back towards Africa. I'm looking right here in America. That's why I feel so good about Booker T. Washington, because I think it needs to be repeated to black people again, "Cast down your bucket where you are Brother and drink deeply of this living water of the American spirit." This is the solution to a lot of our problems. I believe it would increase our participation in civic affairs. Black people are notorious for sitting on the sidelines complaining, but they won't get of their butt and go down and vote and so they are taking no responsiblitiy for what happens except they have full responsibility for not doing anything to make it happen differently. We are in that kind of a situation and so I'm interested in seeing a new generation of black people who are not looking out of America towards anything, but who fiercely embrace their Americaness. And I'm saying to them get involved. Upgrade your skills, get yourself together, go out into America and make it your own.

I believe that instead of black people hating the police department, I think they need to join the police department and take control of the police department and make it our own. I think that black people should join the Army; take control of the Army and make it our own. I believe that black people should get involved with the political process and get involved like they have never been involved before. And I think the time has come where America will listen to black people and will even elect black people to any office and to the very highest office in this land.

Anthony: Why do you think this?

Cleaver: We have a vast reserve in the person of the American blacks who fully partake of the American experience and if properly oriented ideologically will constitute a very powerful formidable force right here in America. It's for those reasons that I am taking another fresh look at my membership in this great organization called the United States of America.

Anthony: Can you give us some of your thoughts about Castro's Cuba, your first resting place in your long odyssey into exile. Is there racism in Cuba?

Cleaver: I think there's not only racism in Cuba but it's a racism that would shock the average American because of its primitiveness. It's the racism we dealt with in the 1890s. It's a kind of hatred and antipathy that I have never really felt to be a part of my reality. It's alien to America, the kind of racim you find in Cuba. But you will find also a lot of classical, very familiar expressions of racism. The population in Cuba is split up into the black Cubans, then there's a mixture of Negro and Indian Cuban, and there's a mixture of Negro and Spanish. You can see all of these different mixtures and the color spectrum in Cuba is quite a fascinating rainbow. I used to tell those Cubans that if they were all in America, they would all be niggers and they would all be classified as niggers, but in Cuba they were nitpicking over different degrees of pigmentation in their skin.

You can see that blacks were manipulated on the color line politically, but the color question there goes as deep as the revolution itself and it was really through members of revolutionary organizations that I found out what was really going on in Cuba.

The authorities who had control of me in Cuba began to accuse me of attending some sort of secret Black Power meetings. I was flabbergasted, because I'd never even dreamed that they even had such meetings in Cuba. Of course, after they accused me of attending them, I started seeking them out to see if they really existed and to find out what was going on. Sure enough, I found some people at the National Library who were members of some groups who were in opposition to Fidel Castro. These people opened my eyes to the racial situation in Cuba and the history of racism in Cuba. They regarded Fidel Castro as a maneuver by the white element to avoid, or forestall a black revolution that had been aiming historically to take control of Cuba the way that Toussaint L'Ouveture took contol of Haiti. Now, that's where his Black Cubans were coming from. So, they look at Fidel Castro as some kind of weird happening in Cuban history, as a plot against them. That's how they look at him and you can see the difference in where your head is if you are coming from there or if you are coming from the Cuban revolution. Now that's the very extreme, and these people told me about groups of guerrillas in the mountains who refused to give up their guns when Fidel came down out of the mountains.

And they also pointed out to me that Fidel Castro put himself at the head of the black revolution that was going on and whose proper leader was Antonio Masseo, which is why I named my son Masseo, because I discovered this great truth. It was my revenge upon the Cubans, naming my son Masseo, because I saw the secret of their lies and their oppression of black people is tied up in the person and the secret of Antonio Masseo, the man who truly liberated Cuba from the Spanish.

Anthony: Tell us more.

Cleaver: Cuba now gives credit to its liberation to a white man by the name of Jose Marti and they have statues of Jose Marti all over Cuba and his image is being paraded all over Havana. They have a big majestic monument outside of Havana tht looks like the Tomb of the Unknown Soldier. It's the tomb of Antonio Masseo and this is the dude that actually liberated Cuba. Antonio Masseo and Jose Marti returned from New York to Cuba in a boat, just like Fidel returned from Mexico in a boat and they landed in about the same place that Fidel landed and they built an army and they marched from one end of the island to the other and liberated Cuba. And they defeated the Spanish.

I say they marched. Antonio Masseo marched because Jose Marti got killed soon after he set foot off the boat. He got blown away and for years Antonio Masseo led the army to final victory and then liberated the army. He was on his way into Havana to be installed as the president of Cuba when one of these whites shot him in the back and killed him. Now that's the secret treachery of Cuba, so that people who were following through in the tradition of the Black Revolution. They have been dying and fighting for decades. This goes back centuries and they do not look kindly upon Fidel Castro or any other white man being head of their government. That's just the way that is.

Anthony: Why did you go to Cuba?

Cleaver: I went to Cuba on a prearranged situation where we had made arrangements with Cubans in New York for me to come there and organize and man a facility that would train our members in how to use weapons, how to make bombs and other demolition techniques and also train us in Marxist political and economic philosophy. We made this deal with them in New York at the United Nations, but after I got to Cuba they wouldn't do it and they gave me all kinds of little phony, corny reasons why they didn't want to do it. And it was only later on that I found out the problem was the impact that I had on the black Cubans. You see, those people they're like that, they're ready to get down like that and they responded to the Black Panther Party just like that. And it was an unsettling thing because we were really unrelenting in our position concerning black freedom, so we would reiterate this to the Cubans and they started calling the police pigs and stuff like that.

But your question goes very deeply into Cuban history. It goes to the very bone of Cuban history where the Cubans don't even know if the majority of the people there are black or the majority of the people are white. The blacks say the majority are black. The white say the majority are white. And you have that kind of a powder keg situation with the whites still maintaining a ruthless domination and control at the top.

Anthony: Is it true that you had an affair with a woman, a Caucasian woman who ws also a mistress of Prime Minister Fidel Castro in Cuba?

Cleaver: This woman was not properly labeled a (mistress) of Fidel Castro. Many people don't know it, but Fidel Castro is incapable of having sexual relations with women. When Fidel Castro was captured by Batista he was castrated along with the other dudes who were captured.

Anthony: Is that right?

Cleaver: Yes. This is why Fidel Castro has no children and Raoul Castro has no children. They cannot deal with women. This is not well known, but it's known by people who know what's going on. There was this young lady in Cuba who went back very far with Fidel Castro.

When Fidel Castro came to the United States after he gained power—that famous episode when he visited the United Nations and his chicken plucking sessions in his hotel downtown, then he moved to the Hotel Theresa in Harlem and met with Robert Williams, Malcolm X and the NAACP and Robert Moore and all of those people. This girl also made contact with him then. He invited her to come to Cuba. And when I got to Cuba it was 1968 and this girl had been there already for a couple of years. Fidel had come in there in 1960. So this was an old story by then. It was three or four years old at least, when I got there. One day I was standing in the line with a couple of these American hijackers that I used to hang out with and I heard a woman's voice speaking English above the din of all that Spanish. I looked around and there was a fairly nice looking woman, a beautiful woman under the circumstances. Speaking English made her really sound great and one of the brothers knew who she was. She lived in the Libre (Hotel) where he lived and so I cut into her and made provisions to talk to her. We started kind of hanging out together a little bit and she told me about her relationship with these people.

Now, what happened was, I was at her apartment at one or two o'clock in the morning. We had been out walking, which we would do a lot. I didn't have any kind of sexual relations with her. And I say that not to say anything except she refused. You prefaced this by saying that I was involved with his mistress. What I'm saying is that I had nothing sexually to do with his mistress. This woman was Fidel Castro's pet and they called her Bunny because she had a little bunny rabbit in her apartment.

Now, in a country where housing was at a premium, you had families living on top of each other and you had families sleeping in shifts, Fidel Castro gave this woman two apartments in the center of town. One in the Havana Libre Hotel and the other in a private complex of apartments which was the tip top. This is like living downtown. It was a choice hotel and a choice apartment that Bunny had and it was about a four room apartment and she hardly ever went there until I came along. She would only go there to feed her little bunny rabbit and Fidel Castro used to send heads of lettuce from his farm everyday for Bunny and her bunny rabbit.

She told me all about her relationship with Fidel and her whole history and I suppose the Cubans felt that this was a threat for me to have this kind of contact. That's all it was to it.

Anthony: That's quite a bit, Eldridge.

CHAPTER XVI

Finally, We All Bled

It didn't take me very long to find out what Huey Newton thought of my interview with Eldridge Cleaver. A week or so after the magazine came out, in March, 1982, I was in the Bay Area and ran into Huey. It so happened I was with Eldridge at the time and that made for a few tense minutes.

Understand that, in spite of the deadly war between the Newton and Cleaver fractions of the Panthers, Huey continued to hold some respect for Eldridge. Being a smart man, he knew that Cleaver had probably saved his life by coming up with the Free Huey campaign and getting him out from under all the heavy duty stuff that was coming down on him in jail.

A few weeks before the interview came out I talked to Huey on the telephone and told him about it. I knew that he read the magazine and would see it, eventually. At the time I probably thought it was best to warn him. Huey was unpredictable. His first reaction was: "What did Eldridge say about me?"

Cleaver did not like Newton's activities, and had gone public in papers such as the Los Angeles *Times,* saying Newton and the criminal element from Oakland ran politics in the city. Cleaver had told me in our interview that Congressmen Ron Dellums, who knew Newton through the

Oakland political scene, had gone down and visited when he was in exile in Cuba on the murder charge of the seventeen-year-old prostitute. Dellums, the tall, handsome, longtime black Oakland/Berkeley Congressman had been a friend of Newton, as had many black city and county politicians in the Bay area.

According to Eldridge, Dellums had asked Newton for the meeting in Havana. His purpose for visiting Huey was to ask him if the Black Panther Party would refrain from running Bobby Seale for mayor the second time in 1977, a race Bobby was favored to win. Instead, Dellums wanted the BPP to support his friend, Judge Lionel Wilson. Newton supposedly agreed and when he returned to the United States to stand trial, he convinced Seale not to run for mayor. The Black Panther Party supported Lionel Wilson, who then became Mayor of Oakland.

Anyway I'd gone to the Bay Area just after the interview was published on business and called Cleaver who lived in Oakland/Berkeley. He invited me over to Fred Ivy's restaurant, in Oakland, that March day. Ivy's was a popular meeting place of political types. It was also a place Newton frequented.

We ate as soon as we got to the restaurant, then went to his car to smoke some dope. Only a few minutes had passed, when Newton pulled up in his luxury car and three black men in long leather coats got out. One was Big Man. He opened the front passenger side door, and out stepped Newton dressed in a white tailor made suit, with cape, and for effect, carrying a cane. The body guards surrounded him as they entered the restaurant. Needless to say, Huey Newton liked entrances.

Cleaver and I followed them into Ivy's and sat down at a table back from the bar. I wanted to compose myself before speaking to Newton, particularly since I was there with Cleaver. It was hard to figure how that was going to play.

I saw Newton walk to the bar and order a drink. The bartender nodded at Newton and said, "I'll be with you in a minute, Huey."

Huey drew back the cane he was carrying and knocked all the drinks off the bar. "I want a drink now!" he shouted.

Huey was served.

I waited until he had finished his first drink before I approaced Huey. We bearhugged. His greeting was warm, but then I had something to offer him as a writer, and he saw me in that perspective. Newton quickly acknowledged he had read my interview with Cleaver, glancing Eldridge's way. I again told Huey I wanted to interview him as well, and I had an assignment to do so. We'd also, in the past, talked about doing a second volume of his autobiography together. The first one had been published in the early 1970s and was called *Revolutionary Suicide.* It had been a Book of the Month alternate selection and Huey had made a sizable hunk of change off it.

Huey asked me to step to his car and I followed him out of the restaurant. Once we were alone, he confided to me that he could not do an interview, because he was "organizing the Party to deal cocaine in Oakland." His reasoning for that activity was, he said, because he wanted to raise money to keep the Panther free school open, and also to restore his vision of political/military revolution in America.

He had made a contact in Cuba to supply the cocaine from Columbia. I really didn't want to hear anymore than I already knew about his cocaine dealing activities. I tried being evasive, hoping to get the subject on another track.

"You need more positive exposure. Like people knowing more about your activities such as the free school, that sort of thing. And about your relationship with your political friends, like Mayor Lionel Wilson for instance," I said. Huey cracked a smile, and tilted his head: "Has Eldridge Cleaver been telling you that I made some political deals on the on that murder beef about the whore?" He asked, smiling. "That sounds like some shit Eldridge would come up with."

So then I stuck my neck out and asked him pointedly if there had been some sort of political deal because Cleaver had told me there had been, and Huey Newton was a free man walking the streets after having exiled himself to Cuba over the murder of the prostitute.

Newton answered: "I've always liked you...and I trust that you will never try to print rumors as fact in a matter like this...but you understand, don't you, that no judge set me free. I was set free by a jury of my peers." Huey laughed. "So whatever Eldridge has told or whatever you've heard in regard to that rumor about my having a deal with Ron Dellums and Lionel Wilson is really beside the point, isn't it?"

He just sat there staring at me with that famous smile on his face. He had me and he knew it. One thing Huey knew about and that was survival."

Newton then opened my world to crack cocaine. Only the very elite had it at that time, and I smoked it from his glass pipe because he told me it was the most dynamite drug ever to come on the market, and he felt the Panthers could make a lot of money off it in the Bay area market. I didn't become a regular user until 1983, because I didn't have a contact, and had to wait until it became popular in the streets. As it would turn out, it became far, far too popular in my street. I developed a major problem with crack cocaine that caused me to lose a lot of friends and almost cost me to lose my family.

Although I talked to Newton a couple of times on the telephone after that meeting, I never actually met with him again to find out if he followed his master plan to deal cocaine. I know he was convicted as a user, and the story through the media about his death by gunfire by alleged Black Guerrilla Family member, Tyrone Robinson, on August 22, 1989 does bring up a couple of questions.

Huey Newton was dead at forty-seven years old. I remember reading, when I was young, the black novelist Willard Motley, who said: "Live fast, die young, and make a good-looking corpse." That would have been a fitting eulogy for Huey P. Newton.

And what eulogy is there for the rest of us who picked up

the gun. We found that trying to make revolution in this country is like spitting in the wind, it will blow back into your face.

I became a serious abuser of crack. That, I suppose, was Huey Newton's legacy to me. For years I'd get stoned because I kept seeing all the dead young men marching in front of my eyes when I'd close them. Little Tony and Bunchy and Steve Barthlomew, Tommy Lewis and John Huggins, shot down at UCLA, Fred Hampton and Mark Clark in Chicago... an endless grave-bound line of young black faces.

There were others. Many others. They weren't all black. Back in those Panther times we had support from a lot of white celebrities. I knew some of them and became friends with one or two. There were others that I knew or heard about. One of those I knew about, but don't think I ever met, was the actress Jean Seberg.

Recently a friend showed me a book, *Played Out,* that had been written about her by drama critic David Richards. Like many celebrities and other idealistic white liberals, she got caught up in the BPP cause. It may seem strange in retrospect that this blue-eyed blonde, All American type actress from Iowa would get involved. But you must remember, we were what was happening! Leonard Bernstein and other of New York's famous entertained us in their homes.

The problem with Jean Seberg was that All American white wasp look from Iowa. Apparently someone in the FBI went nuts and decided to make an example out of her. She had for years been married to the French writer and diplomat, Romain Gary. He wrote a beautiful and poignant obituary in which he accused the FBI of hounding her into suicide. All because she had come out on the side of the BPP. Gary said strange men would call her parents's home in Iowa in the middle of the night pretending to be "Black Panthers" and talk to her folks about having sex with her. Then, when she became pregnant the rumor was spread that the baby was fathered by any of several Panthers.

By the time the baby was stillborn, she was so distraught

she flew home to Iowa with the body and insisted on an open coffin funeral. The poor woman was desperate to prove her baby wasn't fathered by a Black Panther. She killed herself in the back seat of her car, parked on a Paris street. Lay down and went to sleep. She supported social change. She spat in the wind.

We all did.

We all hurt.

We know what happened to Huey. Bobby Seale lives in Phildelphia where he is in charge of a minority recruitment program at Temple University, and has become a successful businessman; he owns a barbeque restaurant, and published his own book a couple of years ago—a cook book! I got permission to run the Eldridge Cleaver interview that appeared in the February, 1982 issue of Players. I think it reveals a lot about the man he had become, then. Eldridge now lives in Berkeley and travels to write and lecture.

Gail is attending Pepperdine University, where she is in the psychology masters program. Upon completion of her studies there, she will become a licensed physchologist.

My stepson, Kante Anderson is nineteen now and is enrolled at San Francisco State University. He is a film study major.

Our daughter, Matt, is attending California State University at Northridge where she is a pre med major.

Me, I've just been trying to keep it together as much as possible. I got help for my crack cocaine problem. Not once, but several times. I had a very lot of help and support from my family and friends. The last time, I feel I managed to get my head together. And then I managed to write this book. It was a painful process.

It hurt.

But today if something hurts I don't find it hard to open my mouth and say:

"That hurts."

Yes, finally, we all bled.